TACTICAL WISDOM

BASE LINE

TRAINING
MANUAL

TW-01

BASE LINE TRAINING MANUAL

TACTICAL WISDOM SERIES

TW-01

JOE DOLIO

ISBN-13: 9798741045060

Preface

The prudent see danger and take refuge;

But the simple keep going and pay the penalty.

Proverbs 22:3

Several years ago, I was going through some very rough times and couldn't find answers to the issues in my life. There were serious personal issues, I had destroyed nearly every relationship that mattered in my life, and our country was rocketing down a dangerous path.

In the midst of all this confusion, I had lost focus and my way. My most trusted advisor, known to many as "Miss Ali", suggested that I try the Every Man A Warrior program at the Church. Me, being a man, and a Marine at that, was rather skeptical that sitting around talking to a bunch of other guys about my problems was going to help at all.

That's where this entire idea was born. As I begrudgingly attended meetings, I met great men who shared their stories and their concerns, and I found that a lot of them were feeling the same way I was and having the same issues I was having. Things started to turn.

The EMAW program taught me to look at the whole Bible, not just the parts that the Pastor shares on Sunday. As I did that, I read it from my perspective as a United States Marine and as someone interested in preparedness and tactical training, and I found great passages and people who illustrated tactical and preparedness truths that are still valid today.

After taking the program a few times, I was asked by a man who has quickly become a great mentor of mine, Bill (I don't share last names, they know who they are and privacy matters), to lead a group. I accepted and as we began the study, some of them found my interpretations of Bible passages and characters from a tactical perspective to be insightful and completely different from what they've known.

As these discussions went on, I recalled a conversation I'd had with Tim, a veteran of the 82nd Airborne. He asked me if I had ever considered writing a blog because of my interesting viewpoints and writing style on social media. At the time, I wrote it off as the usual Army hero worship of Marines, and the general oddities associated with him having been a sniper (just kidding, Tim). I mentioned this conversation to Miss Ali, and she said "You absolutely should".

Thus, Tactical Wisdom was born. It began as a blog discussing tactical and preparedness advice as found in the Bible, with some current events and intelligence sharing, always with an eye towards preparing Warriors for rough times.

Most people see the Bible as a collection of rules to be followed and threats of punishments if you don't. If you get beyond those preconceived biases, there are great adventure stories of epic battles, spies & secret missions, subversion and resistance to tyrannical government, wilderness survival, and solid advice. In my research, I found that most of the tactics used by Nehemiah, who I call the Grand Father of Combat Engineers, are still taught by Western military forces today.

As the blog grew, a few great things happened. First, I got a lot of comments about how my writings had convinced a few people to take a fresh look at the Bible, and that's good enough. Second, a woman who had been away from the Church a long time asked me to help her get reacquainted with Christianity. I considered that a solid win.

The last thing that happened was that a few different people began saying "Man, if you put this in a book, I'd buy it". At first I laughed, but then a few actual authors joined in. When a serious academic writer encouraged me and asked me to help provide content for a book he was writing, I began to seriously consider it.

For almost as long as I've known her, Miss Ali has been telling me that I should a write a book, although I think at times she was being a bit sarcastic. I ran the idea past four men who had been doing Every Man A Warrior with me for years (you know who you are), and they were enthusiastic.

This book is a product of that. I hope that you all enjoy it, and find it as a handy reference as we negotiate these troubled times.

How To Use This Book

This book is designed as a field manual and handy reference. You can read it straight through, or jump to the practical skills you need right away. I suggest reading it straight through once, then go back and do the work.

At the beginning of each section, there is a verse that supports the concepts in that section.

At the end of each chapter is the Base Line Standard, or goal to be achieved.

Finally, at the end is a study of Elijah, a Biblical Warrior who taught a good number of solid preparedness and tactical lessons that are just as valid today.

Get prepared, both physically and spiritually.

Table of Contents

x

Base Line Training Manual

Introduction

The beginning of wisdom is this:
Get Wisdom

Proverbs 4:7a

When we consider the topics of preparedness, it's easy to get afraid, with all of the risks and problems in our society today. The information age was supposed to make our lives easier, but they've made it ever more fraught with risk. We've never been so dependent on electricity and computer networks, and now literally even your sink faucet could possibly be network connected and not work without power.

As recently as the 1950s, every man in America had the skills to build a fire, make a tent out of a tarp, hunt, and have the fortitude to sleep in the wild, even in winter. Do you feel like our current society has this ability? Particularly the younger generation?

At the end of the Second Boer War in Africa, General Baden-Powell was appalled at the lack of outdoor skills his young British Army troops had, since the majority came from the highly urbanized London area. He launched a program to teach young boys military scouting skills and outdoor skills. For this, he developed a book, Scouting for Boys, which is still a highly sought after item today (I recommend downloading a copy if you can find it). From his work, he founded the Boy Scouts, and with his sister, he founded the Girl Guides almost immediately thereafter.

Now, as always happens, both of those organizations have gotten so far away from their original intent, that boys rarely learn outdoor skills anymore, and the girls never do.

However, the creation of the program was borne of the same issue we face today: As a society, we've lost the ability to fend for ourselves. The average person in Western society keeps about 2-3 days of food in their house, is overly reliant on technology to bring them news & communication, and has absolutely no plan to survive any calamity that may happen.

We see it every time a disaster strikes, and people are caught unaware: If only the government had warned us or gotten to us with food sooner or rescued us or whatever. A complete and utter lack of personal responsibility.

Preparedness is exactly that: Accepting that your safety & security is YOUR responsibility, and no one else's. Sure, the government can help, but their response, by virtue of their entire existence, is entirely post-event and reactionary. It's OK to get help from the government in an emergency, but you should never RELY on it.

That's where western society went wrong. The Second World War was a warning and a wake-up call. People had just began to live more urban lifestyles, moving from a rural and agrarian culture to an urban and industrial one, and it began in Europe. Because of that, when the German war machine swept through Europe, no one was prepared to defend against them, and even worse, no one was prepared to survive in the devastation that came after.

If you want to learn about true tales of survival, read about Germany in late 1945-mid 1946. Read about the lives of those who lived during the Troubles in Northern Ireland. Read about the people trying to survive as Yugoslavia collapsed and during the resulting wars of secession and genocide. Talk to a survivor of the

Ukrainian Revolution. Look at what people are doing to survive today in Venezuela.

The biggest lesson from all of these historical (and current) examples, is that the time to prepare and train is BEFORE an event happens. The rampant crime and looting as a result of Hurricane Katrina wasn't due to the storm or the flooding, it was due to a massive number of people who were unprepared and had never given a thought to "what if", despite living in city with a history of both devastating storms and a foreign invasion from the sea. That's the purpose of this book, and this entire series of books.

People imagine that in an emergency, their neighbors and community will pull together to help each other. That may have been true in the 1950s, but today they are far more likely to see that you are more prepared and then come to you for help. If you don't hand over some of your supplies, they will band together and try to take them from you.

As we begin, many readers will think, "but in my area, people won't act that way". This idea comes from normalcy bias, which we will discuss a lot. They won't act that way in the current situation and circumstance. How people might act right now is very different from how they will act on their third week without electricity, fifth day without food, and fourth day of their children not getting food. EVERYONE will act differently under those circumstances.

The information age was supposed to bring people closer together, however, instead it has made it so that no one has to interact with other humans in a meaningful way. Think about this: Just 15 years ago, to get groceries, you had to drive to the store and get them. If you wanted food, other than a pizza, you had to drive to the restaurant. If you wanted the latest widget, you had to go shopping. Now, there is no reason for you to leave the house, if you don't want to, and in fact, you are literally discouraged from doing so, under COVID-19 pandemic rules.

These books are designed to be references for you to use in preparing, and then to be able to carry into the field with you to use as a reference guide.

This book is meant to be the bare minimum standard for anyone looking to begin their preparedness journey. It will be very basic, and we will build on it in later volumes with specific skill sets to help you grow and learn. The series will be skill-intensive, and while we will mention a few specific pieces of gear, they aren't meant to be gear catalogues. You can lose gear, but skills you will retain.

Your most important lesson is that skills are more important than stuff. I can own hundreds of feet of para-cord and dozens of tarps, but unless I know how to build an effective shelter, the stuff is useless. I can buy a $700 medical kit, but I will bleed out unless I know how to use the gear.

This book should also be the basic level for everyone who joins your "Mutual Assistance Group" or whatever you call your band of merry heroes (I don't recommend using the "M" word that's mentioned in the 2nd Amendment - it draws federal agents like unpaid taxes). Yes, you will need a group. Your group could be your family, it could your friends and their families, or a group of like-minded people who band together.

Not only will you need a group, but training together is fun. Getting a group of people together and doing a land navigation scavenger hunt, or having a fire building/shelter building class is fun. We even once got a large group together and had teams camouflage and hide one of their members. It was a great time and everyone learned something.

Our fragile society is never more than 72 hours from total collapse. That's an important concept. Whatever the situation today, 72 hours can result in the world turning completely upside down. Rather than discuss the obvious situations of storms or earthquakes, let me give two other examples of modern western societies collapsing.

In 2008, The Republic of Georgia was becoming a friend of the NATO nations, and a couple of areas wanted to become autonomous. This is analogous to the Pacific Northwest and the rest of the US currently, as an example. Over a few months, the crisis spread, but the majority of Georgia, outside of 2 regions was completely peaceful.

On August 1, as Georgia attempted to stop the lawlessness in her breakaway areas by moving police in, Russia invaded by land, sea, and parachute. By August 7th, hundreds were dead and thousands wounded, mostly civilians, there was no power in most of the nation, and a foreign army and various militias held a large part of their territory. That territory is still occupied today, with repression and targeted killings on both sides.

An even more relevant situation developed in just 72 hours in the Ukraine in 2014.

On February 18th, mass protests against the President began in the capital. The protests were confined to downtown and the rest of the country went about life normally. Does this sound familiar?

When the 19th began, police sealed off the protest zone in downtown Kyiv, and people noticed, but since it didn't affect their lives, they paid little attention to it, since it was just "those kids protesting again". While the TV showed the protestors shouting about "revolution", no one put much stock in their ability to actually do. Again, does this sound familiar?

On the 20th, a state of emergency was declared and over 48 hours, 77 people were killed in clashes in the downtown area. Again, while people were concerned, it was still just those kids in the capital.

By the 22nd, the protestors had completely overthrown the government, and all the fighting had been confined to the capital. The people in the rest of the country woke up to find themselves in a new nation, and armed militias sprung up to resist the protestors, but too late.

The problem for the militias was that they had waited until their government completely fell to try and save it. Now, in the eyes of the international community, THEY were the separatists, when just 72 hours before, they were government supporters.

Fighting immediately broke out and Russia used the confusion to seize an entire region, the Crimea, and most of two others.

The end result: Complete devolution from a modern society to a place with intermittent electricity and water service in less than 72 hours. Some areas have changed hands on a daily basis ever since.

The lesson to be learned is that we don't know what the next 72 hours may bring. The main issue we have as a society is our over-reliance on electricity.

In 2003, a large portion of the US and Canada had a mass power outage from August 14th through August 16th, plunging about 55 million people into darkness. There were widespread issues. It's important to note that in Detroit, the power failure ended on the 18th, but full water safety wasn't re-established until the 20th. There were sicknesses from the water, sewage spill-overs, and transportation issues for days after the event ended.

You CAN minimize the effect of what happens to you during these situations by being prepared. This manual is designed to start you on that path.

At the end of each chapter, you'll find a Base Line Standard. That's level you should maintain as a bare minimum base line.

Let's head down the road and start learning some Tactical Wisdom.

Tactical Wisdom

Base Line Training Manual

Chapter 1

What is Preparedness & What Are You Preparing For?

Be on your guard, stand firm,
Be courageous; be strong.

1 Corinthians 16:13

Have you ever watched one of those "Prepper" TV Shows?

I swear that they intentionally seek out the craziest, most outrageous people that they can find to feature on those shows. Then, they get a camera in their face and ask them "What are you preparing for" and they give some outlandish and crazy scenario. This is by design. It's purpose is to paint prepared people as crazy, because why would you need to prepare for anything in our modern society of immediate convenience and "just-in-time" logistics, right?

The scenarios these people present range from plausible to the outrageous. They say anything from a super-eruption at Yellowstone (which is entirely plausible) to an EMP strike from China to an alien invasion. Some of it is pretty far out there.

The funny thing is, despite their motivation or personal "doomsday" scenario, once they began discussing their preparations, they were nearly identical. All had provided for some food storage and then long term food production, water procurement, shelter, and their own defense.

This led to the development of my own philosophy of preparing for the second and third order effects. My philosophy is not to prepare for any specific scenario, but to be prepared for the second and third order effects of ANY scenario.

Let me explain: When a tornado hits, the destruction is the first order effect. That destruction causes a power outage, which is the second order effect. The power outage means the stores are closed and food spoils, making a food shortage a third order effect. Another third order effect in this scenario is that if you live in a place with municipal water, the pumps will lose power, and your water will not be safe to drink, so water shortage becomes a third order effect.

If you analyze any potential "doomsday" situation, you'll see that the second & third order effects to you are always the same. You will be without reliable power, reliable water, and reliable food sources. You will also not be in a position to rely on the law enforcement/fire rescue authorities as they will be over-taxed already.

So, then, what is this thing we call "Preparedness"?

Preparedness means retaining the ability to sustain yourself free from any outside support or influence. That means the ability to feed yourself, obtain and purify/filter water, protect yourself from the elements, defend yourself & your belongings, and have some quality of life. Yes, quality of life is important, too.

If that is preparedness, then the next logical question is "What are you preparing for?". If I asked 20 people in preparedness, I'd get at least 10 different answers. Everyone, even me, has their own personal scenario that they prepare for.

The important point, however, is that it doesn't matter one bit what you are preparing for. As long as you take steps to ensure that you can obtain food, water, and shelter, and you maintain some capability to protect yourself and your supplies, it doesn't matter one bit why you developed that capability. I assure you that if you prepared to defend yourself against a Chinese invasion, but instead the power grid was hacked and the power is out, you are still in a good spot as far as being prepared.

The key to preparedness is to not prepare for any specific situation, just prepare to be self-sufficient.

Preparedness is all about self-reliance and personal freedom. Food has been used as weapon for thousands of years, as has access to water. By not being prepared, you are exposing yourself to this risk.

When we talk about preparedness, we are going to discuss it from a no-tech standpoint. That's an important distinction that many fail to make, and it could lead to failure in a survival situation. As a society, we are way too reliant on technology, and many in the preparedness community carry that over.

As an example, let's talk about navigation briefly. Many people discuss the benefits of this GPS or that GPS, but the truth of the matter is that GPS navigation relies on the ground stations having electrical power, to tell the satellites where they are in relation to the earth. Once the ground stations lose power, the satellite position reporting will become unreliable, making navigation by GPS hit or miss.

There was a Second Amendment rally in Richmond, Virginia on January 19, 2020. It brought people from all over the state and country to the State Capitol to protest proposed draconian gun laws. Many people involved in preparedness attended. Many reported that they couldn't get a GPS signal at all during the rally, and after the event was over, the US Navy reported that they had been running an ""exercise" just off shore, and part of the exercise was jamming GPS signals. That event alone should illustrate my point.

This doesn't mean I completely abandon GPS, it means I also learn to navigate by paper maps and a high-quality compass. We do same thing with night vision; while night optics are good, the Model 1 Mark 1 eyeball you've had since birth never requires batteries. A super tacti-cool range finder is nice (if you have batteries), but the ability to estimate distance by sight or by mathematically figuring range using the height of objects is better.

As we prepare, we will focus on SKILLS over GEAR.

Throughout this book, we are going to establish a Base Line training level for general preparedness. In order to do that, now that we've defined what preparedness is, we need to define a few more terms and acronyms so that we are all on the same page.

CB - Citizen's Band Radio Service

EDC - Every Day Carry, items that you carry every day.

EMP - Electro-Magnetic Pulse. A burst of electro-magnetic energy that shorts out all grounded electrical components at the instant it occurs. This is traditionally considered in the context of a nuclear attack, but there are other events that cause an EMP, and there are also newly developed EMP weapons. The point is that an EMP will render most vehicles inoperable unless they are very old or lack electronic control modules.

FCC - Federal Communications Commission

FEMA - Federal Emergency Management Agency. Great resource for information at www.ready.gov. Post-Event, however, they may be a help or a source of problems. They have plans that involve forced relocations, required registrations, and temporary firearm seizures. After Hurricane Katrina, 552 guns were seized under emergency orders, and owners had to submit to a new background check to get their own guns back. They also forcibly relocated residents during Katrina.

GMRS - General Mobile Radio Service

GPS - Global Positioning System

FRS - Family Radio Service

NBC - Nuclear/Biological/Chemical. This refers to an attack, whether it by a nation-state or a non-state actor, such as ISIS or Al-Qaeda.

Post-Event - After some type of event or emergency that causes with a temporary or permanent WROL situation.

Pre-Event - Normal, everyday situation. Before a Without Rule of Law situation.

S/A - Situational Awareness. Maintaining an awareness of what's going on around you and understanding how you relate to your environment, such as where threats are.

WROL - Without Rule Of Law. This is a situation where law enforcement services are non-existent. This could be a long-term situation, years in length, like we've seen in the Balkans, or very temporary, such as the nightly situation during the George Floyd riots, or the first week in New Orleans after Hurricane Katrina. The fact is that Law Enforcement has broken down, and you are on your own. This does't mean we ourselves abandon our civilization; God is indeed still watching. It just means that you cannot count on rescue or support from traditional services. I find this term more realistic than those who say things like "SHTF" or "TEOTWAWKI" (The End Of The World As We Know It).

<u>Base Line Standard</u>

- Decide what you are preparing for.

- Commit to learning skills over just buying gear.

Tactical Wisdom

Base Line Training Manual

Chapter 2

General Awareness Skills

The prudent see danger & take refuge,
But the simple keep going & pay the penalty.

Proverbs 27:12

Scenario 1:

John is prepared and trained. He's got everything staged and
ready. Then, there was an event and the power has been out for 3
weeks. People are starting to riot and panic over food shortages,
so John decides to leave the area. He packs the car at night, to
avoid anyone seeing, and he loads up the family and moves out at
first light.

All goes well leaving the neighborhood, but as soon as John turns
onto the main road leading out of the suburb, there is a
checkpoint. John pulls up, like the good citizen he is. The police
manning the checkpoint then seize his firearms, because although
he's transporting them lawfully, they've been "temporarily" banned
for "safety". They also seize his "excess" food under the Defense
Production Act, because they feel that he is "hoarding", which is
prohibited under the DPA.   They take John's excess gasoline in 5
gallon cans for the same reason. They then arrest John on felony
charges of violating the Defense Production Act (it's a one-year
felony).

Scenario 2:

Susie is on the way to work and steps into the local gas station for her usual cup of coffee. She gets a text and looks down to read it while preparing her coffee. As she turns towards the cash register with her phone in her hand, she sees the armed robber spin towards her and the last thing Susie sees is a flash.

Both of these scenarios are plausible. Both could have turned out much differently if John & Susie had been aware and had done some basic planning.

<u>Area Study</u>

The first step to increasing awareness is to conduct an area study. Actually, you will need to conduct several area studies, one for every every area that you frequent.

First, begin with your immediate area. You neighborhood is your inner-most circle of defense, and you will work outward from there.

Make a sketch of your house, showing all rooms, doors, windows, all details. It does't need to be perfectly to scale, but you will be using it to analyze your risks and develop your defensive and security plan. Once you've made a sketch of your house, make a second sketch of your yard, including every feature.

Once you've done this, analyze your sketches, both the house and the yard, and list the 3-4 most likely "avenues of approach", or ways in which someone could approach or attack your house. Develop a strategy to counter-act each of these.

For example, breaking in the front door could be counter-acted with the addition of a dead-locking dead bolt or, for post-event survival, a locking bar. A large window could be defended pre-

event with bars or locks, and post-event with wood panels or steel plates.
From the yard issue, you might consider fencing or gates, lighting, or cameras. In a post event situation, lighting and cameras may not work, so secondary plans may have to be made, like thorny plants, or removing all brush to clear the lines of sight.

Physical barriers are always superior to technology-based solutions like alarms and cameras because our entire premise is a collapse without power. Remember, power outages are always a second order effect in most scenarios, third order in others.

When analyzing these areas, look at them from the attacker's mindset, not the defenders. In other words, consider how you might enter the house or yard, if you were intent on not being seen.

Next, either get an aerial view of your immediate neighborhood or sketch it out. It's pretty simple to print off an aerial view now, pre-event. Look at the neighborhood and make a few notes:

- How can someone from outside enter the neighborhood normally?
- How can you get out normally? Identify at least two routes.
- How could someone who didn't want to be seen enter the neighborhood? Are there woods/streams/paths?
- How could you leave the neighborhood unseen on foot, if you needed to?
- Area there any houses that are known "trouble houses"?
- What about known safe havens (people known to be friendly and willing to help)?
- Is there any critical infrastructure in the neighborhood, such as utility transformers, switching stations, gas line pump stations, or sewer outlet pipes?

- Are there any businesses in the neighborhood or bordering it that may draw looters or crowds (hospital/drug store/gas station/grocery)?

All of these areas should have notes made in your area study as areas to watch.

Consider these issues from a pre-event security standpoint, and a post-event standpoint. Pre-event, I may just be aware of certain issues, but post event, I might convince my neighbors that we need to block off a road with cars, or set up an observation post overlooking the stream that people might use to sneak into the neighborhood.

Put this information into a written format and save it. A great tool and reference for this is listed in the "Resources" section, the "*Sheep No More*" book and workbooks by Jonathan T. Gilliam.

Next, buy a few paper maps of your local area, and any areas you might go regularly. Paper maps are superior to electronic ones, because, remember, no tech can't fail or run out of batteries. I keep an entire binder of paper maps.

You can get paper maps for free from your city, township, or county, usually at the clerks office. The maps they give you are usually more detailed than ones that you can buy. Some of them even go so far as to list sewer drains and power lines, which is helpful for our purposes. I've even contacted clerk's offices several states away and requested free maps and I've never had anyone say no.

I say several copies, because at least one is going to get marked up during your area study. I generally use a second map for day-to-day use, keeping a local map of wherever I'm at that day in my BattleBoard (more on that later).

For your home, as well as any other location you do this for, find out where the nearest police station, nearest fire station, and nearest emergency room are.

Notice I said emergency room, and not urgent care. In a post event situation, the urgent care will most likely be closed. When researching the emergency room, find out what level trauma center it is. This is vital because a Level 1 trauma center can PROVIDE all care, anything below that can INITIATE care. In a post event situation, you don't want to be waiting in a Level 3 center for an air ambulance that may never come to finish treating your traumatic amputation or tension pneumothorax (sucking chest wound).

Once you have determined where they are, mark them clearly on your paper map, and list the address, nearest cross streets, and phone number in written emergency plans. The address is necessary because post event the phones may be down and you may have to walk or drive casualties there to be treated.

It's important to plot these on a paper map, because post event, these are also locations that will draw people, and usually very upset people. They are to be avoided post event at all costs, unless absolutely necessary, to include going out of your way to avoid them while en route elsewhere.

Listing the physical address and plotting a local fire station might seem excessive, because you'd just go to a hospital if you needed care. The reason you need it is that if you are seriously injured, and need help, a fire station generally has paramedics and/or EMT's on staff 24 hours a day and you can get care started there quickly. Post event, they are also likely to be guarded either by police or troops, and you could seek assistance from them as well. From a security standpoint though, remember that ambulances contain drugs, and may draw the worst kind of attention.

When we conduct any planning, we use the PACE model:

P   Primary
A   Alternate
C   Contingency
E   Emergency

With that in mind, analyze your local map and develop four routes out of your immediate area for emergency use. Do this before an event happens, so that you have a plan. You can react quickly if you already know what to do (that's the entire premise of preparedness).

There are a few vital points about route planning.

First, you have to understand the purpose of the interstate highway system. Originally called the "Interstate and Defense Highway System", the real purpose of the system is the movement of federal troops and supplies in an emergency, hence the "controlled access" entrances, that can be blocked in an emergency. Also, in an emergency, the general population will flock to them.

Any route out of the area you plan should avoid highways. They are too easy to block, they will either be blocked by traffic or government forces, and they are ripe grounds for an ambush by those intent on doing harm. We already experience freeway shootings and we aren't even in a post-event situation yet.

Use secondary roads when planning routes. Plan also to cross under or over freeways away from exit and entrance ramps. The reason for this is that if there is a checkpoint to get on the highway, the traffic backup it causes will block your route.

Plan to cross "trunklines", which are usually state numbered highways or major roads, away from a major intersection, to avoid getting caught in any traffic situation.

Plan your routes to avoid trouble areas. In a WROL situation, you don't want to be passing police stations, hospitals, shopping centers, or pharmacies. These will be areas that looting will occur or panicked people will be gathering. Plan for your trip to take far longer than during normal times.

Identify any safe havens near the route. I say near the route, because a safe haven would be a fire station, police station, or hospital that you should be avoiding, but you should always know where the nearest one is.

Once you've identified and planned your routes, drive them at various times of the day, because a road can be empty during the day, but lined with cars at night. After the plans are finalized, drive them every few months in case they need to be changed. I live in a temperate region, so some routes that I would in use in the summer, I would avoid in the winter.

The next step in your area study is gathering information on local threats.

Your local emergency management agency, whether city, state, or county, can generally provide information on what the most likely local weather and natural hazards are.

Learn where your local power is generated and where the water is treated. These will help you understand how long they'll take to fix if something happens. As a side note, once you learn how your water is treated, you may choose to switch entirely to bottled water.

Your local police department most likely provides a local crime map. Monitor this daily or weekly, depending on how often they update their stats. Sign up for a service like Everbridge, which provides you with text and email alerts from any law enforcement or emergency service that you ask it too, so that you can have daily situational awareness.

Use social media and local news sites to identify the people and groups who are involved in local protest activity and start monitoring them daily. You could avoid driving right into a protest by remaining aware to their activity. Sign up for alerts from your local road commission to know ahead of time about road closures.

Once you've gathered all this information, begin a daily "intelligence check-up", checking local weather (never more than the 72 hour forecast), local social media and news sites, and any alerts you've received. This will help you be more aware of the local situation.

This is a brief discussion of a vast topic, and there are more resources in the "Resources" section to help you with an Area Study.

<u>Situational Awareness</u>

Situational Awareness, or S/A, is having a general awareness of what is going on around you and being engaged in the moment. It's so easy to walk around with your head in your phone not paying attention, but that's how bad things happen.

Lt Col Jeff Cooper, a United States Marine, first devised the "Color Codes of Situational Awareness" shown below.

WHITE	Unprepared & unready to take action.
YELLOW	Prepared, alert, & relaxed. Good S/A.
ORANGE	Alert to probable danger. Ready to take action.
RED	Action mode: Focused on taking action.
BLACK	Panic: Breakdown of physical/mental performance.

The goal is to avoid ever being in Condition White, which is completely unaware, oblivious to what is going on.

Condition Yellow is the baseline standard. You want to be relaxed and aware of what is going on around you, so that you are prepared to deal with the threats that may arise.

I'll illustrate this with a quick example.

Mike pulls in to the local convenience store and sees a Malibu backed in, at the far end of the parking lot. As Mike gets out of his own car, he sees three men in hoodies get out of the Malibu, put their hoods up, and enter the store, splitting up immediately. If Mike was in Condition White, he would have seen none of this and it's highly likely that he would have walked into a robbery in progress. Being in Condition Yellow, our hero Mike saw all of this and decided that he can grab an ice cream and a lottery ticket elsewhere.

Did you notice that Mike didn't go in to break up the robbery? Because we aren't the police or the avenging Angel of God. We don't even know that anything was going to happen. The safest course is to go elsewhere. I know, some of you would say wait and watch. To what end? Again, you aren't the police and the media is filled with stories of bystanders getting shot just sitting in their cars. Why not alert the clerk? Because convenience store clerks are acutely aware and that's their problem to solve. It's harsh, but our goal is AVOIDANCE.

A WROL example involves our old friend John. Remember when he was driving and saw the roadblock? His Condition White thinking led to his gear being confiscated. If he had been thinking from Condition Yellow, seeing the roadblock would have put him into Condition Orange, and he would have taken action to avoid the roadblock and thus retained his gear.

You also want to avoid Condition Black, which is panic. Being prepared, having a plan, and being aware helps you avoid that. People who are in Condition White generally move directly to Condition Black, without passing any of the others.

Being Aware of the Goal

One of the first pieces of awareness we need in preparedness is being aware of our role. Our role is our own survival. We are not light infantry, we are not law enforcement. We are trying to AVOID issues. It's easy to imagine, in a WROL situation, your band of merry do-gooders traveling the wasteland, righting the wrongs of a world gone mad. That is how you become dead.

Yes, we can lend assistance if we truly understand a situation and we can be relatively assured of success, but our over-riding rule is SELF PRESERVATION.

It's harsh, but post-event survival is harsh.

Charity

Being aware of our goal leads to the topic of charity. Eventually, someone will come along and tell you how long it's been since they've eaten and ask you if you have anything to share. This is dangerous for two reasons.

First, they could be scouting for someone else to see if you indeed do have food and supplies to spare. They could be looking to determine how good your defenses are.

Second, and even more dangerous, is that if you decide to give a little food to this person, they will be back tomorrow, with a friend. Then on day three, there will be 4 people. Word will spread that you have enough food that you are just handing it out, and eventually, a group of armed people (possibly even from the government) will show up to take it from you.

This is the harsh reality of a post-event society. I understand that many, including myself, have a belief system that includes charity. I get my guidance from my belief system, which actually allows me to strike a middle of the road position.

Right in the Ultimate Tactical Handbook, the Bible, the answer is plainly given.

For even when we were with you, we gave you this rule: The one who is unwilling to work shall not eat.

2 Thessalonians 3:10

If someone wants you to give them food, explain that you don't have enough to just give it out, but in exchange for performing some task, you can give them a small amount. In a WROL situation, there will be a lot of tasks that you can give someone like gathering firewood for you, turning over a few rows of dirt for planting, weeding the garden, digging a new sanitation hole, etc. This allows you to be charitable, while also not being seen as having an excess.

It's important to note that any work you give someone you don't know should never be security related. You don't want them knowing where your fighting position is located, or your hidden supply cache.

It should go without saying that you shouldn't hand them a rifle, and say "Cover the front while I grab a nap". You most likely would never wake up from that nap and if you do, you'll find everything you own gone.

The Tactical Pause

Probably the best awareness thing you can do is to adopt the 'tactical pause'. Whenever arriving somewhere, before exiting your vehicle, take a look around and take in the scene unfolding around you. This isn't an intense study, just a quick overview, looking for potential threats, whether they are human or environmental.

After you exit the car, try to look inside wherever you are entering if you can, to survey the scene. Once you've walked in the doors, step out of the doorway (fatal funnel), and quickly glance around the scene, looking briefly at each person, and identifying potential emergency exits. After you conduct your business inside, take another pause looking out the door before exiting. These pauses add about 10 seconds and could save your life.

As an example, the majority of people shot during the Aurora movie theater shooting were shot because they went back out the exit that they had come in from, which is human nature. Most of them passed several emergency exits, just to walk out past the attacker. Knowing where emergency exits are is a good thing.

A little insider knowledge is that most businesses mark fire extinguisher locations with a red dot on a pillar where one is mounted, or on the door where one is mounted just inside the door.

- Conduct an Area Study on your home and work locations for you and anyone else you might assist.

- Develop the 4 different routes.

- Internalize the PACE method for all planning (routes, communications, food stashes, etc.)

- Identify local information sources and monitor them daily.

- Conduct the Tactical Pause during your daily travels.

<u>Resources</u>

Area Studies:

    Forward Observer, www.forwardobserver.com

Threat Assessment:

    Sheep No More, book & workbooks by Jonathan
        T Gilliam.

Tactical Wisdom

Base Line Training Manual

Chapter 3

Minimum First Aid Skills & Supplies

He went to him & bandaged his wounds,
pouring on oil & wine.

Then he put the man on his own donkey,
brought him to an inn & took care of him.

Luke 10:34

The preparedness skill you will use the most is first aid. The supplies you will use most will also be first aid supplies and bandages. This applies to both pre-event and post-event life.

The issue is that it's a lot more fun to practice making holes in things, than it is to practice plugging holes in things. One will be used more often, though.

Consider this: How many times in your life have you cut yourself? How many times in your life have you gotten in a gun fight? When you compare answers, it becomes pretty obvious that training to handle injuries is a better use of your time.

Anyone who considers using a firearm for personal defense (or any other weapon for that matter) has an obligation to learn how to treat the wounds caused.

Before we get started, understand that there is no substitute for finding a qualified instructor and taking a class. The American Red Cross is a great resource. At a bare minimum, you'll want to take an adult First Aid class, Adult & Infant CPR class, and a Portable AED class. Yes, take the AED class, you may come across one and it's a good skill to have. I retake these classes as often as possible, because like any physical skill, you have to practice.

Another great resource is the Boy Scouts of America. Obtain copies of the First Aid and Lifesaving Merit Badge Pamphlets. They contain excellent training on first aid and rescue.

Nothing in this book should be taken as medical advice and is presented for informational purposes only.

<u>Understanding the Situation</u>

Understand first that first aid skills are a preparedness skill that you can put into use immediately. For some reason, throughout my life, I've come across a lot of car crashes with injuries and I just happened to be passing by, so I was in a position to render aid. Two of the accidents involved major injuries, and one even involved a State Trooper pinned between two cars (fortunately he wasn't too badly injured). First aid skills literally save lives every single day.

The most important consideration for our purposes is to understand that in a WROL situation, waiting on an ambulance is not going to be an option. Wound cleaning will be vital because antibiotics won't be around, and running water may be a luxury you won't have right away to clean with.

In a WROL situation, we will also need to be concerned with illnesses. You won't just be running to CVS to get cold medicine. Having and understanding how to use anti-diarrheal medication can actually save your life in a survival situation.

Another post-event concern that many in preparedness overlook is the need to be able to identify and treat climatic injuries, such as heat exhaustion, heat stroke, hypothermia, and frost bite. When you know what causes these, you will also know how to prevent them.

Field sanitation is another area many don't think about. Field sanitation revolves around dealing with human waste, without contaminating ourselves, our food, or our water sources.

<u>Scene Safety</u>

The first consideration in treating any casualty is to ensure that it's safe for you to help an injured party. Check to be sure that there isn't a risk of you being injured while trying to help. Creating a second casualty doesn't help the first casualty at all.

In a self-defense or WROL of situation, understand that "There is no medicine in a fight". You cannot treat casualties while a fight is on-going. Resolve the tactical situation, then give full attention to treating casualties from both sides.

During an actual, on-going tactical situation, casualties would be expected to move themselves to cover and render self-aid or provide their own security until the tactical situation is resolved.

Understand that this applies to you as well. If as part of a team, you get wounded, you are expected to treat yourself and defend yourself until someone can help you. The same applies to you if you get injured while performing a task; take care of your injuries as best you can until help arrives.

In a self defense situation pre-event, you can't call a time-out to treat your wounds, so remember that there is no medicine in a fight. Defend yourself, then move to cover and look after your wounds. On a side note, in a pre-event situation, you should also provide whatever aid you can safely & securely provide to your attacker. I know, it seems counter-intuitive, but when sitting at the defendants table, having tried to save the attacker's life will go a long way for you.

The last piece of safety is to understand legal safety. Nearly every state has a "Good Samaritan" law, named after the quote above, that legally protects anyone who, in good faith, attempts to provide aid to an injured person, even if you end up doing more harm (it's easy to break ribs during CPR, to grind bones when splinting, and don't even get me started on what can go wrong with tension pneumothorax reduction). An important part of preparedness is to research and know your state's Good Samaritan laws.

In that same vein, in a WROL situation, limitations on treatments that an EMT or paramedic can do in the field go out the window. It's OK to learn to how to run an IV in order to start Ringer's Lactate or Hextend, because in a WROL situation, no one will be asking to see your license. The same goes for learning how to reduce tension pneumothorax (collapsed lung).

<u>Initial Assessment</u>

Most injuries will involve a conscious victim who can tell you exactly what's wrong, or an obvious injury/illness that you work on. Others will require a quick assessment.

The MARCH Algorithm is the best way to remember how to perform an assessment.

M	Massive Hemorrhage/Bleeding Control
A	Airway Management
R	Respiratory Management
C	Circulation/Shock Management
H	Head Injuries

The point is to rapidly yet thoroughly assess a patient to determine what the biggest issue is and go to work on reducing that.
A quick way to apply the MARCH Algorithm is to just start at the head, and work your way down the patient. Lightly run your hands over them, watching for discomfort, and checking your hands after each body part, to look for blood. Look for obvious discolorations and dislocations.

This is a good time to have a notebook handy to write down what you find.

<u>Tourniquets</u>

Applying a tourniquet used to be considered as an absolute last resort measure to stop a bleed. It is now considered a FIRST STEP method.

With an extremity injury, start immediately by applying a tourniquet as high and tight on the extremity as you can, starting with the armpit area or groin area, depending on where the wound is. This is a stop-gap measure, designed to immediately slow bleeding.

Once you've resolved the immediate security issues (won the gun fight if there is one) and completed initial steps of aid, such as applying a trauma/pressure bandage to the wound, you can then move the tourniquet to 2-3 inches above the wound.

Use only CAT or SWAT-T tourniquets, rather than something like the RATS tourniquet. You want something that can be applied one-handed on yourself if necessary.

I recommend have two tourniquets, and that everyone on your team carry them in the same place. This is because when treating a casualty, you should use THEIR first aid kit, not yours. You could carry one tourniquet on your first aid kit, and a second one in a cargo pocket.

Practice applying a tourniquet on yourself with one hand. The time to figure it out is not while your blood is pouring out onto the ground.

Apply tourniquets very tight, past the point of pain. Being in pain is better than dying.

Bandaging

Bandaging is nothing more than just tying or securing a gauze pad in place over a wound. There are many schools of thoughts on this, but this is really all you should worry about.

All you need to do is cover the bandage or pad to hold it in place and keep it clean. Wrapping an ACE bandage, self-conforming bandage, triangular bandage, or bandana around and tying it off is good enough.

If bleeding has been controlled, tie the knot to the side of the wound. If bleeding has not been controlled, tie the knot directly on the wound.

NOTE: In a WROL situation, applying antibiotics and wound-cleaning become far important. Before the First World War, infection was the number one killer in combat wounds.

Medicinal Preparedness

When preparing for a WROL situation, a big area that is commonly overlooked is medications, both OTC and prescription.

We are so conditioned to getting sick, then either dropping by the pharmacy to pick up cold medicine or visiting the doctor, that we overlook it.

We're going to cover a list of OTC medications that you should have stocked, but we're going to begin with a discussion of how to stockpile prescriptions.

The best way to prepare in this area is to get healthy and get fit, which will increase your resistance to all kinds of illnesses and decrease your reliance on medications.
However, there are some strategies to build up a supply of prescription medications.

First, most insurance programs will let you refill at 25 days, when it's written for every 30 days. If you purchased every 25 days for one year, you'd have an extra 60 day supply built up.

Second, a lot of insurance programs allow you to buy a 90 day supply by mail order. Do that as often as you can and you'll also build up a supply.

Third, talk to your doctor and ask for "samples" of your medications. Doctors are given good sized supplies of samples by pharmaceutical companies that they can hand out. If the doctor gives you samples, put those in your stockpile, rather than using them before your prescription.

Store all medications in a cool, dry place, without extreme variations in temperature.

As far as expiration dates, there is evidence that medications retain about 90% of their potency for at least 5 years beyond their expiration date, and many times much longer. However, liquids are NOT as stable. Make your own decisions here.

Here's a list of OTC items that you should have:

1. Hand Sanitizer: At least 60% alcohol

2. Ibuprofen: Motrin/Advil

3. Naproxen: Aleve - Longer lasting pain relief.

4. Aspirin: In addition to pain relief, it is a blood thinner.

5. Acetaminophen: Tylenol - It's the only pain reliever that isn't an anti-inflammatory and is better on the stomach. You can alternate Ibuprofen and Acetaminophen every 2 hours if needed.

6. Diphenhydramine: Benadryl - In addition to it's life-saving antihistamine properties, Benadryl can be used as a sleep aid.

7. Loperamide: Imodium - Anti-Diarrheal medication can save your life in a WROL situation as diarrhea causes dehydration. Changes in diet will lead to stomach issues.

8. Laxatives: Again, changes in diet in a WROL situation will cause stomach issues.

9. Pseudoephedrine: Sudafed - An excellent decongestant, but stockpiling it has been made difficult as it's so controlled, despite being OTC. You need to be careful in building a stockpile, because you could get labelled as meth dealer.

10. Fexofenadine HCl: Allegra - another antihistamine for allergies.

11. Meclizine: Dramamine - This is a motion sickness treatment, which can be used to treat nausea/vomiting. It also helps with anxiety.

12. Hydrocortisone: For wound treatment

13. Bacitracin: For wound treatment

Build up supplies of these, but also resist the temptation to use OTC medications on a daily basis, because your body builds a resistance and reduces the efficacy.

Finally, let's discuss Amoxycillin. There is an on-going debate about whether or not fish antibiotics can be used by humans or not. The answer is "it depends". If you buy it in capsules, then yes. There are some powders that are mixed with things meant to help fish only, but if you buy the capsules, they are quite literally the exact same capsule.

To illustrate this, I did an experiment. I went and purchased the fish capsules, and compared them to pharmacy-supplied prescription Amoxycillin that we had on hand. They were the exact same capsule. Again, make your own decision, as it's your body.

<u>Minimum Base Line Individual First Aid Kit (IFAK)</u>

Keeping the MARCH algorithm in mind, your basic first aid kit should contain all the items needed to resolve the issues on that list. Here are the minimum requirements for anyone:

- CAT or SWAT Tourniquet (avoid RATS Tourniquet)

- Trauma Pressure Bandage

- Trauma Pads/ABD Pads

- Chest Seals or Occlusive Dressings (at least 2)

- Rolled Gauze

- Gauze Pads (4x4 & 3x3)

- Clotting Agent (Quik-Clot/Cellox)

- Medical Tape

- Duct Tape

- Nasopharyngeal or Oropharyngeal Airway (with lube)

- CPR Barrier

- Gloves (Nitrile is better)

- Triangular Bandage

- Self-Conforming Bandage (ACE-type)

- Triple Anti-Biotic (either wipes or tube)

- EMT Shears

- Casualty Blanket/Space Blanket

This is just the minimum.

On a side note, there should never be anything in your first aid kit that you don't know how to use. If you don't know how to insert an NPA (nasopharyngeal airway), learn how. If you don't know how to use a chest seal/occlusive dressing, don't rely on reading the package during an emergency, learn how.

When buying things like triangular bandages (which you can never have too many of) or self-conforming badges, try to buy them in dark colors, like green or black, rather than traditional white. You have to consider that in a WROL situation, you may not want to be seen or found. Consider the same with the casualty blanket, most civilian ones are silver on one side and orange or red on the other, but you can find them in OD green or camouflage on one side.

Some extras if you have the space and skills to use them:

- Hemostats

- Tweezers

- Forceps

- Hydrogen Peroxide (either small spray bottle or wipes)

- Alcohol wipes

- Needle for tension pneumothorax reduction (NEVER attempt unless you've been trained)

- Aspirin/Tylenol/Motrin/Benadryl/Anti-Diarrheal medications

In addition to your trauma kit, you should also develop a "boo-boo" kit, containing a variety of bandaids and some alcohol wipes. You'll use this kit more often, but it's helpful to have. The most often overlooked item is fingertip and knuckle band aids, so I always buy extra.

Make several kits and put one in each car and one in each bag you carry.

Every time that you use something from the kit, replace it IMMEDIATELY. If you wait to replace it, you'll find yourself without it when you need it. The obviously necessitates having an extra supply of all components, mostly of band aids. It is recommended that you keep the extra supplies in a transportable bag, so that in the event of a major event, you can just pick up the supply bag and go. Ammo cans work well for this as well.

Some people carry much more and some more advanced items, but this is the Base Line kit that you should never be without.

Another recommendation is that you put the major trauma items all in one zip-lock bag, and the boo-boo kit items in another so that in the event you need to treat yourself with one hand, you can just grab the larger zip-lock and then pick out what you need from that, rather than trying to root through a larger collection of items.

<u>Base Line Standard</u>

- Build a personal Individual First Aid Kit

- Build a personal Vehicle First Aid Kit

- Own at least 2 Tourniquets

- Obtain Adult CPR/AED Certification

- Be able to:

    - Apply a Tourniquet

    - Bandage wounds

    - Apply a pressure dressing

    - Splint an extremity

    - Conduct a MARCH assessment

<u>Resources:</u>

1. American Red Cross: www.redcross.org
2. National Safety Council: www.nsc.org
3. Boy Scouts of America: www.scouting.org
4. Local fire and health departments

Tactical Wisdom

Base Line Training Manual

Chapter 4

The Bare Minimum - Supplies

The woman fled into the wilderness to a place prepared for her,
Where she might be taken care of for 1,260 days.

Revelations 12:6

The guidance in The Ultimate Tactical Handbook isn't bad; that's enough supplies for just about 3 and a half years. That's a good goal to strive for, but may be a bit much for those just starting out.

Unlike most books on preparedness, we aren't going to focus on firearms. Those are an accessory. There are four areas that you need to take care of before you get to defense:

1. First Aid - Without adequate first aid supplies, you may die and nothing else you do will matter.

2. Shelter - Without shelter in a rough environment, you can die almost immediately.

3. Water - Without water, you will die in 3 days.

4. Food - Without food, you will die in 3 weeks at the latest.

The most important survival knowledge you can have is the "Rule of 3's":

- You can survive 3 minutes without air (or in icy water)

- You can survive 3 hours without shelter in a harsh environment

- You can survive 3 days without water

- You can survive 3 weeks without food (as long as you have water and shelter)

Our goal should be to mitigate these risks as quickly as possible.

We already covered first aid, so let's discuss ways to mitigate the next three items.

<u>Shelter</u>

One of the first purchases you make should be tarps. Yes, tarps, plural. Tarps have many survival uses including shelter, protecting supplies, camouflaging positions, and water collection.

There are a multitude of tarps in various shapes, thicknesses, materials, and colors. For our purposes, we have a few requirements:

- We generally want them in 9'x12' size or larger. You can always fold it to make it smaller, but you can't stretch it to make it bigger.

- It needs to be waterproof, not water resistant.

- It should have reinforced grommets at more than just the four corners.

- It should be in an effective camouflage pattern or an earth tone. An unfortunate side effect of a WROL situation is that there will be bad folks out there looking to do bad things, and you should use every advantage to hide yourself.

Military tarps are a great option as they are reversible and can be snapped together to make larger shelters, but they are often rather expensive.

A required accessory for owning tarps is either Gorilla Tape or camouflage duct tape to make repairs that will be water proof.

Side Note: MacGuyver was not wrong when he said you can do almost anything with duct tape.

With tarps, you'll need some type of cordage, like para-cord, to tie the tarp into a shelter. You'll also need some type of tent stake, such as the large "nail-type" stakes. A good idea is to start with 8 stakes and go from there. You can keep both the stakes and cordage in a US Military surplus tent stake bag or other similar sized bag, stored right with the tarps, or even with them tied around the tarp so that you can just "grab and go".

Once you get a tarp, get out into the field and practice setting up various types of shelters using the tarp, the most basic two being a lean-to and an A-Frame. The time to learn isn't during an emergency.

To make an A-Frame:

- Select two trees and tie a piece of cordage between them. This will become the center ridge-line of your tarp. Don't make it too high, remember we are trying to remain concealed.

- Lay the tarp over the ridge-line with equal amounts of material on each side.

- Pull the sides out and stake them down, so that they are tight. You can either stake the tarp directly into the ground, or use cordage to suspend them above the ground, for ventilation.

- Make sure you leave enough room for your gear to be inside and out of the weather, and enough room for "self-administration", like changing clothes or washing.

To make a Lean-To:

- Select two trees and tie a piece of cordage between them. For a lean-to, this should be higher than on an A-Frame, but only as high as you need.

- Tie the tarp to the cordage.

- Stake down the rear directly into the ground.

- You can fold in the excess from the sides if you have extra material, and use your gear to hold it down, creating a windbreak, if necessary.

Tarps can also be used as top cover over your tent or a ground cover under it.

Tarps are a vital tool and you need at least one, preferably several.

Tents are also a good tool for shelter. The tendency is to want to buy a giant, cabin-type tent for comfort, but since in this volume we are discussing the bare minimum, the recommendation is a small backpacking tent.

A small, 3 person backpacking tent is really about the right size for a single person and their gear. Resist the temptation to buy one that you can stand up in, we want to be low-profile.

A small basic 3 person tent has enough room to sleep, store your gear out of the weather, and conduct self-administration inside of it for one person. Any smaller is really too small.

When selecting a tent, color is again important. They don't often come in camouflage, but if you shop around, you can find them in earth tones like tan, brown, or green. Avoid the brightly colored ones. Winter is the best time to shop for one, as the price is generally the lowest then.

Another feature of the 3-person backpacking tent is that it is lightweight, quick to setup, and generally fits inside of or attached to your ruck.

Even after setting up the tent with a rain fly, it is helpful to spread a tarp between the trees above it and a little larger, as added weather protection.

Once you find the right tent, don't just store it away with "your stuff". Practice setting it up (more than just one time) and taking it down. The training standard you should strive for is to be able to set it up in under 5 minutes in the dark and take it down quietly in the dark within the same timeframe.

You also need some type of sleep system, such as a sleeping bag. The best way to do this is to buy a three season sleeping bag. If it is too warm, you can sleep on top of it, and if it's colder than the bag is rated for, you can wear extra layers as you sleep. It's OK to be cold at night; humans survived for millennia without four-season sleeping bags.

Many experts recommend some type of sleeping pad to isolate your body from the ground. They are bulky, and take up space, and they are generally pricey. A compromise, if you can attach it to the outside of your pack, is a yoga mat of decent thickness. They make them in black and they roll up, usually with straps, which you can then attach to your ruck.

The "Ranger Roll" is a tried and true item that actual field veterans swear by. This is a US military poncho and poncho liner tied together. The poncho liner comes with strings attached to tie through the grommets on a standard US poncho. When tied together, this makes a good moderate weather sleeping bag. You can either keep the two separate and attach them each night, or keep them separate so that you can use the poncho during the day.

You can insert a casualty reflective blanket between the two for early spring and late fall, and if you also add a US wool blanket in the middle, it becomes a four season solution.

My personal set up is to have two US ponchos, one in a ranger roll and the second on the belt for use as needed as either a poncho, or as a tarp shelter.

The US Military Issue poncho is truly the Swiss Army knife of field shelter. You can wear it to keep you dry, you can make a ranger roll sleeping bag, you can use it as a tent, and it has double sided snaps so that you can attach several together to make a larger shelter. As an added bonus, it comes in the ubiquitous woodland camouflage pattern.

And, for prepping on a budget, if you aren't wearing camouflage and suddenly need to, due to circumstances you encounter and you want to avoid contact, you can throw the poncho on over your clothes, wearing the hood and you are now in full camouflage. Everyone should own at least one.

At a bare minimum, you need either a small tent or a tarp/poncho with cordage and stakes to keep you out of the weather.

Water

Most experts recommend about 3.7 liters of water per day for adult males and 2.7 liters a day for adult women. That's roughly a gallon for drinking, per person, per day. This number doesn't take into account vigorous physical activity.

This doesn't include washing yourself or clothes.

As you can see, storing enough water is going to be a problem. Water is bulky and heavy. It's far preferable to have a method to purify water, rather than to rely on storage.

It's a good idea to have a short term supply of water, like 2-3 weeks, but you should be considering how to sanitize water, rather than storing a huge supply.

Obtain some type of water filter. You can go online and spend days reading posts about which one is better or why this particular one is best but literally ANYTHING is better than nothing. On day 183 without water service, I assure you that you aren't going to care what brand water filter it is.

Get a filter system that can go a long time between filter changes or one that is self cleaning (plunger type ones).

It's a good idea to have a larger filter for use in a static location and having a portable straw or plunger type one for your use while moving on foot, like evading or patrolling. Redundancy is the key.

Without a filtration system, there are still things you can do. Bringing water to rolling boil for a full minute is still the best way to make water safe (please wait until the water cools completely to drink it). Before boiling, however, a good idea is to pour the untreated water through a coffee filter first, to remove larger sediment.

You can also make water safe using bleach. When using liquid bleach, never use anything but plain bleach at 5.25% to 6% sodium hypochlorite content. For each gallon, stir in 1/8 of a teaspoon of bleach and let it stand for 30 minutes. It should have a slight chlorine smell and taste.

Another option is water treatment tablets. They come in small bottles or strips. They are available anywhere that camping supplies are sold. They're a bit expensive, so a good idea is to buy a small supply of them, along with a filter. You can use the tablets when you have to grab water from a stream on the move, and the filter when you have more time.

You can use buckets or tarps to collect rainwater, but it still needs to be treated or boiled.

The key to water is learning where to find it in your local area, and having a method to treat it, of which boiling it still remains the best method.

A recommended base line is two military-issue canteens and a 100 Oz/3 Liter water bladder. The canteens should be on some type of battle-belt system, rather than attached to your pack. If they are attached to your pack and you have to drop the pack for whatever reason, you now have no water.

Somewhere, also on your belt, should be a supply of water purification tablets. The reason is that while boiling is the best solution, you can't rely on having the time to boil water and you may not want to have the signature of a fire. Tablets allow you to quickly fill your canteens from a water source, drop in the tablets, and keep moving. The tablets don't care if you are moving while they work. If you are using US military issue canteens, the issued belt canteen pouch has small pockets meant to hold water purification tablets.

It is also recommended that if you are using the issue canteens, you buy at least one canteen cup, and one canteen cup stove (preferably two of each). Both are meant to fit with canteen inside them, inside the belt pouch. My personal set up is that both canteens each have a cup and a stove attached. There is virtually no weight added and now you have two cups and stoves for cooking.

In recent conflicts, the United States Army has gotten away from canteens, in favor of traveling with large quantities of bottled water. The Army is far more mechanized than the US Marine Corps, and has a significantly larger logistical tail that can bring water everywhere they go, so they've gotten away from it.

The US Marine Corps, however, exists to operate from the sea with only what they can carry with them, so Marines have always trained to carry two canteens on their belt, rather than on their pack. You may have to drop your pack, but you'll still be wearing the battle belt, with your water and some water purification tablets.

The Marines also have the institutional memory dating back to the Solomon Islands. When the Marines invaded Guadalcanal, the Japanese resistance was so fierce that the US Navy was driven away from the beaches, along with nearly all of the USMC's supply chain. General Vandergrift and his Marines were alone on island, with only the supplies they had with them, and they remained there, cut off, for months. Doesn't that sound like the scenarios we envision in a WROL situation?

You can't rely on a static supply of long-term water storage, because you may have to flee and water is too bulky and heavy to transport.

The solution, then, is portable storage and purification capability.

Food

A caution before we move into food…we're going to kill a couple of the sacred cows in the preparedness community, so be warned.

When first beginning in the field of preparedness, your first storage goal should be two weeks of PORTABLE food. Yes, portable. Many in the preparedness field suggest buying giant bulk size containers of food. That may be a good idea once you've set up a SECURE bug out location, but for a base line rule, you need two weeks worth that is portable.

Regardless of whatever type of event you foresee and are preparing for, you need to understand that in any crisis, the ability to get up and move with virtually no warning time and exist for a short term on what you are carrying is vital. Portable food, whether it is MRE's, backpacking food, or canned food, is the way to begin.

Buy and try out a few brands of backpacking food and find something you like. It doesn't have to be your favorite food; in a survival situation, you'll eat most things, but if you don't like SPAM, don't buy it.

When buying canned food, again stay away from giant bulk-size cans. Many swear by them, but you have to consider what you will do if you aren't ready to eat an entire 5 pound can of green beans in one sitting. You most likely won't have a way to preserve the food in open cans.

An easy way to develop a two week supply on a budget is to buy 3-4 extra cans of food on each shopping trip. The added cost is negligible, and you will quickly build up a supply.

Once you have a two week supply, set a new goal, maybe one month. Then 3 months, and so on.

Here's the next sacred cow we're going to slaughter: You shouldn't be trying to store a 10-15 year supply of food. If you can, and have the room, feel free, but what we're going to work on is infinitely better.

After accumulating a 3-6 month supply of food, you should being working on a permanent ability to PRODUCE food.

Humans existed for millennia before modern food storage methods made going to the store more convenient than producing your own food. They did this by hunting, fishing, gathering, and growing. Those skills aren't lost; you just have to develop them.

Learning to plant and grow food is a super-power, and the ability to store that harvested food is what meant some cultures survived and some did not.

When buying seeds, you want to try for heirloom varieties, as they are tried-and-true, and can be stored forever. Avoid hybrid varieties, as they are engineered to produce more food, but do not reproduce as efficiently as heirloom.

Learn what local plants are edible, so that as a last resort you can forage and gather plants and fruits.

Fishing gear should always be part of your emergency supplies. Once we are in a WROL situation, fish and game law enforcement will be pretty low on the priority list, and if you live near water, you can have drop lines in the water constantly, producing protein literally around the clock.

Growing up, I learned this lesson from my grandfather, who had three lines running on the river bank all day, every day, and always had fresh fish.

Learning to trap is another great skill to have. You can set up snares, and just like the fishing lines, snares will produce protein for you around the clock with minimal effort. However, if you are going to set snares, check them daily. You don't want to be feeding the local coyote or hawk population.

Hunting is an absolute given in a WROL situation and should be considered as an ongoing activity, rather than something you go out to specifically do, as you do now. Whatever other activity you are doing, you should be prepared to take game at any time.

Think about your life. How often do you come across wildlife when you aren't specifically trying to, like when out for a walk? It's more likely to happen by chance than by specific goal, so always be in a position, unless actively trying to evade someone or trying to avoid making noise, to take any game encountered. Again, enforcement of game laws will be low on the priority list, and preservation of life takes precedence.

Once you have set up a 2 week supply of portable food, developed a 3-6 month supply of stored food, and have developed your capability to produce food, then you can begin to worry about buying larger quantities of stored food.

Several people at this point are probably thinking, "But I plan on bugging IN, so I don't need portable food and I need a large bulk supply". There are a few issues you need to consider first:

- If you are bugging in and you are the only person in the neighborhood who isn't losing weight or actively seeking food, someone will come and find out why, probably forcibly.

- You could still be forced to move. Rioting, looting, and arson accompany WROL events. Having some portable food would enable you to hide for a few days and then come back.

- The Defense Production Act: The DPA allows the government, in a declared emergency, to seize things that you have a large supply of, such as food, if the government decides that you are "hoarding". That determination is left up to the local emergency manager. You could also be charged with a felony.

- During the 2020 COVID-19 State of Emergency, large quantities of surgical masks were seized using the DPA and the man who owned them was arrested by the FBI under the DPA, despite the masks being legally purchased by him.

- FEMA may force you to relocate with only one bag per person. This happened during Hurricane Katrina in New Orleans.

In addition to food storage, you need a portable way to cook food. MRE's come with MRE heaters, but you need an additional resource.

Backpacking stoves and fuel are a great idea. Most are reasonably priced and generally come with a cook kit that stores the stove inside.

You'll also need some type of small can opener, like the ubiquitous P-38 can opener that you can take with you. Some type of field eating utensil, like a tactical spork or plastic knife/fork/spoon set is another often over-looked item.

<u>Base Line Standard</u>

The following is a recommended base line standard for preparedness, and something to achieve before moving on to larger goals.

- Some type of portable shelter.

  3 Man backpacking tent

  Tarp/stakes/cordage

  US Military Issue Poncho Shelter

  Preferably all three

- Portable Sleeping System

  3 season sleeping bag

  "Ranger Roll" system

  Possibly an isolation/yoga mat

- 2 Canteens/Water Bottles

  With at least one, preferably two, canteen cups & stoves

With belt pouches to hold the system

- Portable filter/straw filter and/or water purification tablets

- 2-3 weeks stored water

- Optional: 100 Oz/3 Liter water bladder

- 2 Weeks of portable food

    Canned/vacuum sealed/dehydrated/MRE type

    Some type of can opener, like a P-38

- Portable stove and cooking system

- Mess kit of some type

Chapter 5

Basic Survival Kit

...fill the men's bags with as much food as they can carry,
And put each mans silver in the mouth of his bag.

Genesis 44:1b

That wisdom from the Ultimate Tactical Handbook is certainly a good start.

In this chapter, we're going to discuss the contents of a basic survival kit. This is NOT your bug out bag or anything like that. It is designed to be thrown into your bag.

This kit isn't designed to sustain you indefinitely, it's designed to support life with the bare minimum. In the next few chapters, we'll build on the bare minimum kit and work our way up to a full-size long-term sustainment ruck.

This kit should fit in a gallon sized Zip-Lock bag or smaller. We're talking the absolute bare minimum for survival. It's a good idea to have more of these items on hand, but resist putting them in your survival kit. The purpose of this kit is to make it small enough to be conveniently carried everywhere you go. If it becomes too large, you won't carry it.

Another option is to have one small one, and a few larger ones. For example, I have a personal survival kit inside my daily carry bag, and a larger survival kit in the car. Both have the same baseline items, but the car kit, since it's not designed to be carried everywhere, has a bit more of the same items.

<u>Fire</u>

You need some method, and preferably a few, of starting a fire. You have a few options, and the best kit contains all three.

Matches are a tried and true item, and a staple of preparedness. Buy windproof or stormproof varieties. These can be found with waterproof storage containers that have striking surfaces attached. These windproof/stormproof matches are waterproof, and long-burning. They are a great item to have. Refill boxes of these matches can be purchased and kept on hand.

You can make your own waterproof matches by soaking kitchen matches in turpentine or clear nail polish, or by dipping them in wax, but it's generally easier now to just buy them already waterproof.

Avoid the paper matches, as they have never been very effective, get wet easily, and don't burn very long at all.

A lighter is a good addition, but it will only work for as long as you have fuel. Disposable lighters are fine, as long as you understand that they are a SUPPLEMENT, and you should still have other methods for starting fire. Lighters are mechanical, which means that if the wheel or flint breaks, it is useless.

A better second solution is a ferroceum rod or flint and steel. Basically, the rod is struck with a metal blade, causing sparks to fly into a pile of tinder. These work well, no matter the weather, and they have a long service life. Some come with a bar of magnesium to assist in igniting tinder, but that's not a necessity.

If you get a rod or flint, practice a bit in using it and you'll see that it's simple and effective.

A supplement to these materials is some type of easy-start tinder, which is sold at outdoor stores. This is a small supply of material that will light no matter how wet, and is a good idea to have as well, as long as you only put a small amount in the kit, to keep it small.

Another good item to toss into the fire kit is a small handheld pencil sharpener. You can insert a stick and twist it as if you are sharpening a pencil, and you'll make a pile of very fine tinder, that is easy to light.

You can also collect some pencil shavings or dryer lint into a small plastic baggie for use as tinder. Ask your local fire department how many house fires are caused by dryer lint; you may be surprised at how easily it burns.

Water

For a survival kit, we're not too concerned with carrying water, but we are concerned with obtaining water.

You can buy a couple of small bags of survival water, which has long shelf life, but remember that water is heavy. These survival bags are typically 4 oz.

You should have some type of straw filter or purification tablets in order to purify water. Most straw filters also come with a collapsible water bag to store a bit of water.

You can also find, at outdoor stores, collapsible water bags that you can stored rolled up inside your kit, only opening them when you need them to save space. Mine have carabiners attached so that when full, you can attach them to your gear or belt. You can then roll them back up when they're empty.

In a pinch, an empty Zip-Lock bag can be used to store water.

<u>Shelter</u>

For the small survival kit, we aren't looking to carry a tent or full shelter.

A survival blanket meets this need nicely, because you can sleep in it, or you can set it up as a reflector, to retain the heat from your fire.

Having a 50-75' length of para-cord in your survival kit doesn't take up much space, but it can be used to build a survival shelter from natural materials. You can also use it to set up a survival blanket as a shelter.

There are several survival sleeping bags and tents on the market that are very small, and are made of the same material as a survival blanket, and they make good shelter items. The only issue from a WROL standpoint is that these typically only come in bright orange, to facilitate emergency rescue. In a WROL situation, we may not want to be easily found.

Understand that these are short-term survival items, and they aren't a replacement for more permanent gear in your other kits.

<u>Food</u>

While we are going to put a couple of food items in the survival kit, we aren't going to be concerned with carrying food here, we are concerned with procuring food from the environment.

For stored food, a couple of protein bars is a good idea. A small amount of chocolate or hard candy should be kept in the kit as a quick way to boost sugar levels, and they both have long shelf-life.

On a side note, hard candy prevents coughing, which can help in a survival situation for security.

The first food procurement item is fishing gear. Not a fishing pole and a full tackle box, but some fishing line and some hooks, sinkers, and maybe a lure. One option is to get a small reel of line, and just put it in the kit, but have several hooks already set up on leaders and swivels.
Several hooks on leaders can also be used to slow pursuit during escape & evasion, but that's a topic for another book. It's mentioned here to point out that your gear should always have more than one use. Sinkers could also be used in a slingshot to hunt small game.

Your kit should also have spool of small wire for setting snares. What I recommend is getting floral wire from a craft store, as it's coated in green plastic, which protects the wire from water and camouflages it for snares. Once you buy snare wire, learn how to set snares and practice them. The time to learn is never in the middle of a survival situation when failure means you don't get to eat.

Medical

It's important to note that you should have a completely separate first aid kit that should always be with you. In this discussion, we're only going to mention items in addition to that kit that you should never be without.

You need a few small pill bottles with Aspirin, Acetaminophen, and Ibuprofen for minor aches and pains or fever reduction.

You need in your survival kit a supply of anti-diarrheal medication. In a survival situation, diarrhea is a life and death matter. You will most likely already be dehydrated and diarrhea will dehydrate you even faster. Obtain a supply of some type and put it in your kit.

Another often over-looked survival medication is an anti-histamine, like Benadryl. You may not be allergic to anything that you know of, and still have a potentially fatal allergic reaction. As a side benefit, anti-histamines can be used as a sleep aid, but only use them if you are in a secure situation.

If you're traveling in area where Malaria exists, some medication to prevent that should be carried, along with insect repellent.

A small boo-boo kit of various band-aids can be in this kit as well as the first aid kit, as you can never have too many band-aids.

Other Gear

A commando saw or a small folding hand saw are a nice item to have, and the commando saw takes up almost no space. A commando saw is section of sharpened wire between two finger rings that you can use to cut wood and small trees for fire or shelter.

A folding hand saw takes up a bit more room, but can cut larger items. A good trade off is a commando saw in your personal survival kit and a folding hand saw in your car kit or sustainment kit.

A small sewing kit is more important than many think. If a raincoat or poncho rips, it's useless to you. You can repair small rips in your clothing and gear with a very small sewing kit.

Some type of small flashlight should be in your survival kit. There are a myriad of options here, but get something small and not too bright. Your ultra-bright tactical EDC flashlight should already be on your person, preferably on your belt. You can never have too many flashlights.

For your survival kit, some type of small compass is needed as well. Ball compasses or smaller lensatic ones are a good, low cost option for survival kits. You can also buy a watch compass for EDC, which is a small compass that attaches to your watchband. I have watchband compasses on all of my watches.

As a side note, your watches should be something that is either self-charging or solar, like an Eco-Drive. You won't find watch batteries in a WROL situation and watches are useful for survival.

Knives - The Three Blade Rule

In your everyday life, you should have available three blades:

- A folding pocket knife

- A fixed blade knife

- A multi-tool

If you have these three with you, there aren't many tasks you can't handle from survival to hunting to self-defense.

For that reason, I don't mention them in context of a survival kit, because you should always be carrying these 3 in some way, however your local laws allow. The fixed blade may need to be stored in the vehicle, but it's still available.

If you choose to include a knife in your survival kit, make it a Swiss-army or Boy-Scout type with several different blades and tools.

Recap

Remember, when building a survival kit, start small. Keep it to a small enough size that you will actually carry it daily and that you can toss it from one bag to the next. For example, if a disaster struck while you were at work, and you had the kit in your "Get Home Bag", once you made it home, you could pull the survival kit out of the "Get Home Bag", and toss it into your "Patrol/Bug Out Bag".

If you are tempted to make it larger, make two kits; a smaller one to carry with you, and a larger one for the car.

<u>Base Line Standard</u>

- Build a survival kit as described above

- Carry it everywhere

- Obtain at least 1 folding knife, 1 quality fixed blade knife, and 1 quality multi-tool

- Learn your local and state knife laws

- Develop a method to carry a tactical light with you everywhere you go. For example, I have a leather belt holster that holds a flashlight and a multi-tool.

Tactical Wisdom

Base Line Training Manual

Chapter 6

The Get Home Bag

He said to them, "But now if you have a purse, take it, and also a bag;
and if you don't have a sword, sell your cloak and buy one."

Luke 22:36

There it is, straight from the Ultimate Tactical Handbook. Jesus set out the bare minimum gear for traveling the road. A bag of supplies, some cash, and a way to defend yourself.

In the time that the passage was written, traveling on the road was a dangerous affair. There were bandits waiting along the road to rob you, forces from various factions and movements openly fighting in the countryside, as well as hungry and desperate people who might do crazy things. And, by the way, they were being hunted by the local and national government at the same time.

This sure sounds like the conditions we are concerned about in a WROL situation, doesn't it?

The Get Home Bag is a bare-minimum bag that you should carry or have available anytime you are away from your house. It will contain some bare minimum gear to allow you to travel, on foot, from a location that you are stranded at, like work, for example, to home.

In our modern society, we are working at greater distances from home than ever before. It's not unusual to have a 20-40 mile commute to work. Since we generally spend at least a third of our day at work on most days, we should have a plan to get home.

Before we get to the Get Home Bag, let's discuss the other place we spend a lot of time; our cars. Americans have a particular attachment to their cars, and we spend a lot of time in them. That being true, we should have certain items in our vehicle for preparedness. We should consider this the "Vehicle Kit" and keep it in the car at all times. It could be kept in a duffel-style bag, preferably with a strap, so that if needed, you can carry it cross-body, while still wearing your Get Home Bag on your back.

These are good items for a Vehicle Kit:

- Tarp, for use as a shelter

- Wool blanket

- Siphon pump (to get gas if the power is out)

- Pry bar (for moving rubble or light rescue)

- Full First Aid Kit

- Rain gear

- A change of clothes

    - Change into sturdy, outdoor-type clothing in earth tones or dark colors, depending on your environment

  - Good quality boots (Most work shoes aren't conducive to survival)

- Some cordage

- Light Sources

    - A heavy duty flashlight & batteries

    - Battery operated work-light

    - Consider candles

- Non-perishable food, like a few canned items or power bars

- Water, like a US 2 QT canteen

These should be kept in the car at all times, and checked often. With these, you could survive even a remote vehicle accident until help arrives. These are supplements to your other preparations, not a replacement. Never decide not to carry a Get Home Bag, just because you have a Vehicle Kit.

The bag you use as a Get Home Bag should be a nondescript backpack-type. Nothing too overtly tactical, like camouflage, unless that's very common where you live. You can't go wrong with a large, plain-black backpack. Even one with MOLLE-webbing is fine, because nearly all backpacks now have it.

Let's talk backpack fit, because the average person who carries a backpack, does it wrong. We're raising a generation of kids who will develop back problems because we let them carry backpacks to school for years improperly. A backpack is exactly that, a BACK pack...it's not meant to dangle off your shoulders and hover around your lower back, bouncing and swinging. Put on both straps and pull them tight, pulling the backpack tight to your back, with the weight held against the body and high, rather than hanging low and pulling on your shoulders.

Another pet peeve is watching people in action movies, running through an action sequence with a backpack slung over one shoulder. That's silly, as it requires using one of your hands to keep the backpack from falling off, defeating the entire purpose of carrying a backpack. You also see that in business world, with the prevalence of backpack-style laptop bags and everyone carrying them by one strap only. A backpack comes with two straps for a reason, use them both, especially in a survival/tactical situation. If the bag has a sternum strap, use it.

It's a good idea to select a backpack that also has a carry/drag handle on the top, between the straps. If you have to take it off to fit through an opening, it's easier to carry with a purpose-made handle. Also, if for some reason you need to lift it up a vertical surface or lower it down, you can attach a line there.

Now that we've discussed fit and selection, let's discuss what goes it in and how to use it.

My personal bag is also my daily business bag, since all I generally need for a day's work is a laptop, a file folder, and a clipboard, I've incorporated those things into my Get Home Bag Gear.

The first item to consider is a bulletproof panel. They are available at a very reasonable cost and could protect you in your daily travels from an active shooter situation, or in a WROL situation by at least covering your back. The panels are NIJ level IIIA and they slide right into the laptop sleeve of your backpack. My personal choice is actually a bulletproof laptop sleeve from Premier Body Armor. It holds my laptop and actually has two level IIIA panels. The sleeve is always in my Get Home Bag, even if my laptop isn't.

Bulletproof panels are FAA-Approved for carry-on luggage, so that's an added benefit - allowing to you at least be protected at an airport.

- Food - You should keep a few energy bars in the bag, along with maybe some type of pouched protein like tuna or chicken packets you can buy at the grocery store. These are MRE-Style with long shelf life and very small packaging. These types of things can be eaten while on the move and without needing to cook or start a fire.

- Water - You should have some type of hydration in the bag, whether that's a Camel-bak (takes up a lot of space) or a water bottle. You can find collapsible water bottles at outdoor stores, which can be stored empty, but filled in an emergency and attached the outside of the bag. You should have some type of water filtration/purification inside the bag, like tablets. The tablets come in a very small bottle.

- Sillcock Key - A sillcock key is a small 4-way tool, available at any hardware store, that enables you to open the water faucets on the outside of commercial businesses. This is a vital item for urban survival and should be in the Get Home Bag.

- Shelter - The best option here is a US military poncho. It's both rain gear and a shelter if needed. It can also be a sleeping bag. The bag can be folded or rolled up very small for storage.

- Cordage - 75-100' of para-cord is lightweight and small. It can be used to set up shelter or for many other tasks.

- Blades - The 3 Blade Rule applies here. Normally, your pocket knife would be on your person, and your fixed blade would be attached to the outside of your

Get-Home Bag. When using the bag for everyday carry, that might not be an option, but you can store the fixed blade knife inside the bag, and move it to the outside if a survival situation develops. The Multi-Tool could be kept in a pouch on the outside of the bag at all times. Some people store the fixed blade knife in their car, to avoid issues with carrying knives at work, but that may put you at risk of not having it when you need it.

- Duct Tape - In addition to being a great way to cover small cuts, there are thousands of survival uses for duct tape. Take a small amount and wrap it around an old library card or something similar so that it can be stored flat.

- First Aid Kit - A small, self-contained trauma kit, along with a plastic Zip-Lock bag full of band-aids should be in your bag, preferably in an outermost pocket.

- Fire Kit - Some method of creating fire like a lighter, waterproof matches, or a fire steel should be in the bag.

- Socks - A change of socks is a survival necessity. If you are forced to rely on your feet to get you home, you should take care of them. Keep a change of socks inside a Zip-Lock bag in the Get Home Bag.

- Jacket - A windbreaker or packable jacket is a great item to have in the Get Home Bag, not just because of weather. If I need to quickly change my appearance, throwing on a jacket is quick and easy. There are many styles that are made to be "packable" by folding inside of their own pocket. Earth tones are best to blend in.

- Pain Medication - Some type of OTC pain medication in a small tube is a good addition.

- Hygiene Kit - In a survival situation, hygiene prevents illness. Keep a small hygiene kit inside your bag. Inside, have hand sanitizer (either gel or wipes), wet wipes, and a small travel toothbrush/toothpaste.

- Gloves - Some type of gloves to protect your hands are important. Additional liners can be included for warmth in colder months.

- Radio - Some type of radio, at least to receive is essential. The local government will broadcast emergency information via local radio stations. A two-way radio is never a bad idea. Review the Communications chapter for more information.

- Navigation - Keep a paper map and a compass in the Get Home Bag. Learn to use a paper map & compass. In an emergency, if the cell service is down, your phone GPS may not work, unless you've already downloaded a local use map (hint - do that today). This map should be pre-marked by you from your earlier Area Study, listing areas to avoid and areas where you can find help. If you belong to a mutual aid/mutual assistance group, you could have members' locations on this map for emergency aid.

  - You may be tempted to replace the map and compass with a GPS.....don't. GPS is a supplement, not a replacement. As a reminder, during the 2020 Second Amendment March in Richmond, Virginia, the US Navy jammed GPS signals in the area.

- Batteries/Battery Pack - Carry spare batteries for any electronic item, including specialized batteries like radio batteries, and a power-bank type for charging cell phones. Even when cell phones won't work on voice, text messaging may work. A solar power bank is ideal or a larger, portable solar panel for recharging your power bank can be used.

- Paper - One of the most overlooked items in preparedness planning is paper. There will be things you will want to record and document. You should have a notebook and pen/pencil in your Get Home Bag. There may be notes you want to write.

    - As an example, you may want to leave a note on your desk or vehicle to anyone who may come looking for you describing where you went and by what route. Index cards are more durable than paper.

    - If a confrontation occurs during a WROL situation, even though the police may not respond, you are still going to want to write down the details of what happened including date/time/location data, in case rule of law is re-established and you need to defend your actions.

    - Writing is also a way to calm yourself in an emergency.

    - Rite In The Rain makes a great line of products that are waterproof.

    - Paper can also be used as tinder.

- Observation - Some type of small binoculars or a monocular that lets you examine things from a distance is needed. Just small 10x25 binoculars are all you need.

- Signaling - You need some type of way of signaling. A small mirror or a whistle are good options. Chem-lights are also a good way to signal your mutual assistance group as long as every member knows what each color means.

- Shemagh - These are a great multi-use item. You can use it as a dust mask, concealment, a warming layer, a wrap to change appearance, or as a bandage. For urban use, a plain black one is best.

- Hat - At least one hat. This can be a baseball cap, or a boonie-type hat for sun protection. Having two hats allows you to change appearance.

These contents will easily fit into a decent sized backpack.

By reviewing your local area and situation, you can adjust the items as needed. Keep in mind, this is a baseline. You can add extra, but remember that each item adds weight.

A lot of these items are interchangeable between your various bags, so a good idea is to make "modules". Essentially, you get a small container, whether that's a MOLLE pouch, or something similar, and place the items of a specific category in the them.

For example, a fire kit could contain matches, fire starter tinder, a fire steel or ferroceum rod, and a lighter. That's placed inside it's own small zipper pouch and now it can easily be removed from one bag and tossed into another. First Aid kits are the same way.

An "admin kit" could be a small MOLLE pouch (they specifically make admin pouches) that holds a notebook, a few pens, a mechanical pencil, and some index cards. Rite In The Rain also makes notebook covers designed to hold their notebooks and a few writing tools.

<u>Base Line Standard</u>

- Build a Get Home Bag

- Keep the bag with you, or at least in your vehicle, throughout the day

- Maintain the bag, adjusting items seasonally

- Build and maintain a Vehicle Kit

Tactical Wisdom

Base Line Training Manual

Chapter 7

The Belt Kit

The Jesus asked them, "When I sent you without purse or bag, did you lack anything?"

"Nothing", they answered.

Luke 22:35

Sometimes, in a WROL situation, you may want to move around your property or some other location, without a backpack. You may have cached you backpack to move around quieter on a patrol, or you may be working on something.

Having some type of belt set-up for daily wear in a WROL situation can ensure that you are carrying at least a bare minimum of gear to keep you alive.

In the military, this is referred to as the Second Line gear or things worn on some type of load bearing equipment. In our discussion, we'll be using the term "belt", but you could also be using some type of load bearing vest as well.

My personal set up is a USMC issue "war belt", but any type could be used, even the old tried and true "LC-1" belt and suspenders that the US Armed Forces wore from Vietnam through the Cold War. It's recommended to use a load bearing belt that also has suspenders, so that the weight is carried by the whole upper body.

The suspenders also secure the belt to your body (the weight could cause a belt to slide down).

The below set up is a typical one, but by no means the best. Build your belt, and then experiment with what works best for you. One point though is that if you belong to a mutual assistance group, everyone should carry ammunition and first aid gear in the same place.

The first and most important item on a belt for the adults in your group is a personal defense weapon and spare ammunition. In a WROL situation, each adult should have & be trained in the use of a handgun. Basically, put a QUALITY holster on your strong side, and at least two spare magazines on your support side. The weight will balance each other out.

Many people prefer a "drop leg" holster, but most don't wear them properly. Most people wear them too low and too loose to be effective. If you choose to wear one, wear it as high as you can, without interfering with your belt. If it's the kind with two leg straps, only use the bottom one and make it as tight as possible. Just remove the top one.

If you aren't wearing a holster on your belt, because you're wearing a drop leg holster, still leave that slot empty on your belt, so that nothing can interfere with your draw.

In front of the holster on your strong side, only small items should be, so that they don't interfere with drawing. One option could be a pouch for a multi-tool and another for a tactical flashlight.

On the support hand side, behind your spare magazines, it's recommended that if you carry a rifle or carbine, your keep one open-top speed reload magazine pouch for the long gun. The way, if you are just wearing the belt, you could at least have one spare magazine.

Also on the support side, you should put a fixed blade knife. If you have a bayonet, which really just a multi-purpose fixed blade knife, it should go here. When putting a knife on the support side, insert the knife into the sheath with the cutting edge facing forward, rather than behind, as you typically would. This tip comes the ancient Samurai, and it allows you to immediately slash during the draw stroke if you reach over with your strong hand. If drawing with your support hand, you'll have the knife in a reverse grip, also ready to slash as you draw.

On the strong side, behind the holster, you can mount small items, like a tourniquet and a self-defense tool like an expandable baton.

On both sides, behind the hips, there should be a canteen or water bottle holder. I use US issue canteens. Between the two sides, there should be at least one canteen cup and one canteen cup stove. This leaves you the ability, should have to drop your pack and survive off the belt, to heat food and boil water for purification. Ideally, you could have two of each. There is virtually no weight to add the extra.

On the back, somewhere between the canteens should be a first aid kit, both major trauma (blow-out kit) and a boo-boo kit. Again, if you belong to a mutual assistance group, this should be in a common place that everyone knows to check. When another member is hurt, you use THEIR first aid kit to treat them, rather than your own.

In the center of the back, a butt-pack or general purpose pouch should be placed. This could hold a poncho, a survival kit, some cordage, and food. I personally use a USMC Eagle Industries butt-pack, which has a large waterproof central pouch, and three outside pouches. This allows the middle outside pouch to be the first aid kit, one side pouch for a radio and spare batteries, and another side pouch for food. In the main pouch, there is a Shemagh, a US issue poncho, cordage, a note book, camouflage gloves, hat & face mask, and room for more food or other equipment for the day. Other things include a compass and map, or similar items.

This isn't necessarily your ideal setup, but it is a highly functional one. Experiment and make your own set up, but then train by wearing it around the house or property while doing daily tasks, to see if you need to make adjustments or if you can handle the extra weight.

The purpose of the belt system is to enable you carry survival and security gear, while keeping your hands free for other tasks. It designed to allow you to survive if you have to go on the run without any other gear, so set it up with that in mind.

You could leave off the butt-pack/large pouch, if you you knew you weren't leaving your base/home that day, but it's a risk.

To balance carrying more than you should, understand that in a WROL situation, the belt is a supplement to a Patrol Bag/EDC Bag that will have more of the same things in it. It can also be supplemented by a chest rig set up that holds more ammunition, and generally holds your land navigation gear.

Essentially, the belt would only be worn alone around your living location, whether that's your home, a bug out location, or a campsite in the field. If you were "outside the wire", either conducting a patrol, foraging for food, or whatever, you would take a Patrol/EDC bag with you as well.

The point is that you should be able to survive short term with just the belt, and a few days longer with a Patrol/EDC bag, and then even longer with a "full ruck".

<u>Base Line Standard</u>

- Large, padded belt system with suspenders such as a battle belt/war belt

- At least 32 oz of water storage on the belt (preferably 64 oz)

- Holster and spare magazines for a personal defense firearm

- Fixed blade knife or bayonet (Spend a little extra, it's vital)

- First Aid kit storage on the belt

- Ability to carry miscellaneous gear (like a survival kit) on the belt.

- Train in wearing the belt and moving in it.

Base Line Training Manual

Chapter 8

The Patrol/EDC Bag

But the wise took flasks of oil with their lamps.

Matthew 25:4

In addition to the gear on your belt, in a WROL situation, there are other things you should always have at hand, if you aren't inside a fixed location. The best way to carry these is in a backpack, because you can wear it and still have your hands free.

When you first read the list, it may seem a bit excessive. We are not talking about a "current world" situation, but a WROL situation, where you don't know if you'll need to leave immediately with just what you have on your back.

Just like the Belt Kit, the Patrol/EDC bag should enable you to survive for a short period, 48-72 hours, with no other supplies if you absolutely have to. The supplies do you no good, unless you wear it everyday. Keep the weight and size down to ensure that it's not too burdensome.

This bag is not a full-sized ruck, that would be too much to carry on a daily basis. There is a tendency to put more and more things in the bag, but resist the temptation. If the extra items are needed, take something else out. Use the module system discussed regarding the "Get Home Bag". If you won't need cold weather gear, but need observation gear, take one out and put the other in.

Some call this a "Bug Out Bag" or an "Assault Pack". I choose the term Patrol Bag, and I alternate between a USMC Assault Pack and a Highland Tactical "Apollo" bag in ATACS Camo, depending on the terrain and season. The name doesn't matter, as long as you have one, and, once the WROL situation occurs, carry it with you EVERYWHERE. You don't need to always wear it, just have it within arms reach if you are performing a task.

As we get into it, you'll notice that there is a lot of similarity between this bag and the "Get Home Bag". They could conceivably be the same bag, as long as you change the configuration post-event from Get Home to Patrol Bag. In my case, it's two different bags, because post-event, I'm not going to worry about going gray-man, I'll be carrying a camouflage pack and heading into a rural area. The Patrol Bag is set up and ready, and all I'll have to do is switch a few items from the Get Home Bag to the Patrol Bag, which can be done in seconds. Conversely, if I need a black bag for night operations, I'd use the Get Home Bag as a Patrol Bag. Be flexible.

As reminder, no matter what gear system or bag we're talking about, as you use things, immediately re-stock the item as soon as you possibly can. If you went on a two day patrol and ate all the food in the bag, and used several band aids, re-stock the bag with food and medical supplies immediately upon return, before doing anything else.

Just like the "Get Home Bag", proper wearing and fit are essential. Ensure that the bag fits high up on your back, and that the straps are tightened so that you are carrying the weight high on your back. Having the pack tightened properly is vital when you are wearing a backpack along with a war-belt/battle-belt. The pack should touch the rear pouches of your belt system, but not cover them. If you have a sternum strap, use it.

Let's get down to the essentials: What goes in the bag. Remember, this bag is geared to a WROL situation, where the potential for violence without law enforcement support or injury without medical support is real. What may seem excessive to carry today, certainly isn't when there will be potential hostile parties around.

1. Pistol/Rifle Cleaning Kit: In a situation where defensive firearms can save your life, maintenance and upkeep is vital. Carrying defensive firearms, especially openly in weather, can lead to the need to maintain them daily. This gear should be with you at all times. We're not talking about a full box-type kit, but a small cleaning kit; military issue type.

2. First Aid Kit: If you're getting the idea that first aid is important, it IS. First Aid is really a misnomer, because in a WROL situation, it's ONLY AID. I know that we already said you need one on your belt, but a second one on or in your Patrol/EDC Bag means you can help someone else. Put a small one with a boo-boo kit and at least a pressure dressing, along with some duct tape/medical tape in or on the bag.

3. Food: Your Patrol/EDC Bag should some more food, to enable you to last longer in the field if you need to. A good baseline for the Patrol/EDC bag is two "cut-down" MRE's. A "cut-down" MRE is one removed from the packaging, which is mostly air. You can duct tape the meal parts together, but keep the snacks and drink mixes loose. You could use power bars in this bag or pouched-type food (I would avoid cans). If you are going to carry backpacking dehydrated foods, just remember that you will need extra water.

4. Stove/Fuel: Some type of small backpacking stove and fuel, so that you can heat food without a full fire. I avoid the gas-type ones in this bag, due to space, and instead an Esbitt Stove with solid fuel block. Make sure you wrap the solid fuel blocks in a couple of plastic bags if you do this, because they smell like fish. Remember matches to be able to light the stove.

5. Gloves/Hat: It's usually cooler at night year-round, so in the Patrol/EDC bag, keep a watch cap and some gloves.

6. Camouflage Mask/Face Paint: You need both. Many people opt for a camouflage mask or a neck-gaiter type of item, but even with a mask, areas of skin will still be exposed and it may get too warm if you are moving to wear a mask. High-quality face paint is also insect repellent. Get some and learn how to properly apply it.

7. Signaling Kit: Some method of signaling should be in the bag. Either a signal mirror or a whistle is helpful, both is a good idea.

8. Shelter: A poncho or tarp, with cordage (like para-cord) and possibly some tent stakes should be in the bag.

9. Sleep System: Since this isn't a full ruck, a poncho liner or wool blanket would be sufficient; maybe with a poncho to wrap it in. It's a good idea to keep this in a dry-bag; I use a USMC small dry bag.

10. Thermal Tarp: A thermal tarp is a tarp on one side and reflective material on the other. You can use this to reflect the heat from a fire toward you, or as part of your sleep system for warmth. One that is camouflage on one side could be used to place over your position, and in addition to hiding you from overhead observation, the thermal tarp

will hide you from infrared detection tools, like FLIR (forward looking infra-red).

11. Spare Underclothes: You should have an extra t-shirt and underwear, along with a couple of pairs of socks in a plastic bag inside the pack. You could also store it in a dry-bag (I use another USMC small dry bag).

12. Rain Gear: Either a full set of rain gear or a poncho. I have both, but the I only use the poncho as a shelter, and I wear Gore-Tex rain gear. A Gore-Tex jacket also makes a good windbreaker.

13. Writing Tools: A notebook and pens/pencils to take notes/ write notes/etc. Again, Rite In The Rain makes great tools In this area. You'll be surprised how much stuff you might to write down or sketch.

14. Fixed Blade Knife: While you already have one on your belt, you could keep a more "camp" style knife attached to your pack. Alternatively, you could attach a larger machete type knife here. The key is to have some type of fixed blade knife.

Optional Items - If you have the space and weight available, these are "nice-to-have" items:

1. Hand Saw: A small folding hand saw can help gather wood for fire-making, or clearing fields of fire from a position.

2. Small Shovel: Full folding shovels are bulky and best for your full-ruck set up, but a small, folding or take-down hand shovel can be a good help, especially for field sanitation.

3. Snivel Gear: Snivel gear is a Marine term for long underwear. You can carry silk-weight in the summer, and a little heavier in the winter, if you have room. This is mostly for when you are stationary, because when on the move, it will be too warm. Don't forget the thermal balaclava; it can make cold weather sleeping bearable.

4. Spare Clothing: If you have room, a full change of clothes can be in the dry bag with the undergarments. Avoid jeans; they are the worst option for survival because they are restrictive and shrink when wet.

5. Axe/Tomahawk/Hatchet: Another good tool for gathering wood or clearing lanes.

It seems like a lot of gear and a lot of weight, but it really isn't. Build the bag, and then experiment with it, getting the weight and balance right.

Keep in mind, this is the bag for general security patrolling or EDC. If you were going out on a specific task, you'd take things out or add things in to meet the needs for your specific plan, but these should be a bare minimum.

There will be a tendency to want to put in more "comfort" items, but you can't carry everything. Get used to the fact that in a WROL situation, you will frequently be cold, tired, and hungry. Being uncomfortable is expected.

Once a WROL situation begins, this bag should always be within reach. That may seem a bit excessive, but you can't predict when you may need to leave quickly. Remember, in a WROL situation, you won't be calling 911 and waiting for the cavalry. You will either stand and fight yourselves, or withdraw and hide, coming back at some other point.

Our goal is NOT to be light infantry, but to survive.   Never be so tied to a location that you can't pack up and leave. You can always come back after the danger has passed.

In a WROL situation, most of the groups of refugees will just be looking for food handouts, but some will be dangerous, seeking to take things from others by force. These groups are what we are worried about. They will be mobile, looking to raid a place for supplies, and then leave and head back to their own location or camp. The problem is that they are impossible to differentiate at first.

This is the reason we would consider leaving, letting them look for what they want, and then come back after they've gone. Yes, they will take some of your things, but if you've cached most of your hard supplies and are working on food production, rather than on food storage, they won't set you back much.

If you decided to stay and fight it out and lost, they're going to take a lot more than your food.

Action movies showing these grand last stand battles where the virtuous survivors outlast and defeat the marauding motorcycle gang (why is it always motorcycle gangs?) are exactly that, movies. They are fiction. Combat is not fun, especially when you can't just call in artillery or an air strike, and there is no quick reaction force flying in by helicopter.

The Patrol/EDC bag gives the opportunity to survive for a few days if you have to.

Remember also that this book is our bare-minimum standards. In later volumes in this series, we will be discussing how to mount resistance to these groups and other threats, and how to proactively prevent becoming their target, but in this manual, we're concerned with the base line of survival.

<u>Base Line Standard</u>

- Some type of Patrol/EDC backpack

- Secondary First Aid Kit in or attached to the bag (can be the same one you use for the Get Home Bag)

- Portable, field type cleaning kit for your personal defense firearms

- Method of heating food without an open fire (stove and fuel)

- Portable Food - Backpacking/MRE type

- Rain Gear (more substantial than what is on your belt kit)

- Temporary Shelter - Poncho/tarp

- Comfort Items - Spare clothes/socks/warming layers

Chapter 9

The Full Ruck

Gather up your belongings to leave the land,
You who live under siege.

Jeremiah 10:17

The next line of gear is a full rucksack, or "Ruck". In the US military, this is referred to as the "sustainment load" and that's a good description. This line is meant to sustain you in the field for a long term. It contains extra gear for longer-term field survival.

This a full-on "bug-out bag", in my context, and you'll find that my definition varies from some others in the preparedness field. What a lot of other consider a "bug-out" bag is really what I call the Patrol/EDC Bag. The reason for this difference is that I recommend having two separate bags, as most recommend just one.

In the US Marine Corps and the US Army, field troops carry both bags. Their "ruck" contains their long term sustainment gear, and the "assault pack", which is really a patrol pack, attaches to the full ruck. When they arrive at a "patrol base" or temporary camp (we will discuss in later volumes), they drop the full ruck and switch to a patrol pack. This is the same concept we'll use, because it makes sense.

In keeping with this, the Patrol/EDC Bag is the bare minimum for survival, and the ruck contains the comfort/long term gear.

<u>Selecting a Ruck</u>

The full ruck should be a framed pack. I prefer internal frame packs, but the old school large ALICE pack of the US military is one of the best backpacks ever made.

Look for a capacity of around 70 liters, with a bare minimum of 50. You want to be able to carry a good amount of gear in this bag. Get one that is designed well.

A hip belt is a key requirement to help distribute the weight better and to hold the pack closer to your body. A padded hip belt is better, and a padded hip belt with pockets/pouches is the best.

My personal choice is a US Marine Corps ILBE system, which is two bags, a full ruck and an assault pack. The bags are both designed by Arc'Teryx, which is an excellent outdoor company. I choose this because more than any other service, the US Marines live out of their rucks. The Army lives out of vehicles, but Marines are true light infantry, living with what they can carry on foot.

The ILBE system is designed so that you can attach the patrol pack to the outside of the ruck, and it has straps and pockets on the side to hold a backpacking tent on one side, and a sleeping pad on the other side.

The other feature of the ILBE system is that there are waterproof dry-bags designed to fit both bags. This is an excellent resource and I recommend dry bags in any ruck. As a side note, even if you have dry-bags, still keep items you want to keep dry in a ZipLoc bag inside the dry-bag. It may be raining when you want to take something out and this protects your gear.

You should seek a bag with at least straps on the side for holding your backpacking tent and sleeping pad.

Just like with the other bags, proper fit is vital. Wear it with the sternum strap closed and use the hip belt. Tighten all straps to secure the bag to you tightly.

<u>Ruck Color</u>

There is a debate about whether you should have a camouflage ruck or a solid colored one.

Obviously, we always want to steer away from bright colors, and if you choose a solid color ruck, I recommend earth tones, like khaki, olive green, or brown.

The debate exists because many people misunderstand the "Gray Man" concept. The Gray Man concept states that you should blend in and be completely unremarkable, so as not to draw attention to yourself.

I agree in principle with this, but not when it comes to a full ruck. A Get Home Bag absolutely should be a Gray Man type of bag, but when you are moving in a WROL situation, carrying a full ruck, you will stand out no matter how Gray Man your gear is. Full WROL movement is not a time for Gray Man tactics. Gray Man tactics are for the evasion and intelligence gathering in an urban environment.

Consider the environment we are discussing, a WROL situation. People will be scared, uncomfortable, and hungry, and seeing someone wearing a full ruck will mean food and supplies, no matter what color you choose.

With this in mind, I recommend a camouflage ruck. The reason isn't just that it'll be harder to see when I am moving, but rather because if I'm attacked, or if I need to move quickly, I can hide a camouflage ruck in the brush much easier than a light gray, or a dark blue one.

If you notice that you are being followed, you can stash the ruck, then lead the people following you away, returning to get your ruck later, after you've lost them or dealt with them.

Also, a standard tactic in patrolling is that you carry the ruck to your patrol base (a temporary camp), stash and camouflage the ruck, then continue on to your objective without it, returning after mission completion to retrieve the ruck.

<u>Gear Included</u>

1. Sleep System: Some type of a sleeping bag system should go in the bottom. You could use the US Military modular sleep system or any good quality 3 or 4 season sleeping bag. Spend some money here, because you get what you pay for.

2. Sleeping Pad: If you use some type of sleeping pad, it should attach to the outside of the ruck.

3. Tent/Tarp: Your shelter system, whether it is a tarp or small backpacking tent should go inside or be attached to the ruck. The USMC ILBE system allows the tent to be attached to one side.

4. Spare Clothing: A change of clothes should kept inside a ZipLoc bag. Depending on the length of time you plan to operate out of the ruck, you may want a second spare set.

5. Socks/Undergarments: A couple of changes of t-shirts, underwear, and socks should be in their own small ZipLoc bags.

6. Cold Weather Gear: Seasonally dependent, you may want to include a set of thermal base layers year-round.

7. Sweater: If the weather could get cold, a wool sweater is good addition. The US Military wool sweater is good option. These will retain their warming properties while wet. They come in black and green. As a side note, the Army & Marines wear these differently. The Marine way is proper: When wearing a camouflage uniform, the sweater goes over the T Shirt, & the camouflage top goes OVER the sweater.

8. Cooking Gear: Some type of small backpacking stove with fuel and a mess kit is invaluable to allow you to have hot food without an actual open fire.

9. Food: Enough extra food for the length of the planned foot movement or until a planned re-supply happens.

10. Survival Kit: The survival kit you built earlier should be in the ruck if you're using it.

11. Tools: As long as the bag isn't too heavy, attach some basic tools to the outside, such as a camp axe or a collapsible shovel. In a team, each person could carry a different tool, so that you have a variety available.

<u>Living Out Of A Ruck</u>

In the field, you will be living out of the ruck, so it's important to keep it's contents neat and organized.

When in the field, only take out what you need, and keep everything else packed. This way, you can pack up and move with minimal effort and noise.

As an example, keep food and mess gear at the top. Then, when you stop for a meal, you only need to get out what you need to prepare your food and eat.

A security note though: Once you get out what you need to prepare a meal, conceal your bag nearby.   If something happens while you are stopped to eat, you can leave, hide yourself, and then come back later for the bag.

When you stop to camp, get out only your mess gear, eat, and then get out the gear to set up camp after putting away the mess gear. You want only the minimum number of things out at any one time.

Set up your tent or tarp just before you are going to use it, and take it down immediately after use, even if you are using the same campsite for more than one night. The reason is that in a WROL situation, you need to be able to walk away at a moment's notice, with all of your gear.

If a hostile party bumps into your campsite, you won't have time to take down your tents and gather up your gear. You don't want to leave them all your cool-guy gear.

<u>Base Line Standard</u>

- 50-70 Liter size Ruck, with either an external or internal frame

- Backpacking stove and fuel

- Sleep system of some type

- Shelter System - backpacking tent or tarps (or both)

- Survival Kit

- Extra clothing

- Cold/Wet weather gear

Tactical Wisdom

Base Line Training Manual

Chapter 10

Organizing a Team

Two are better than one; they have a good return for their labor ..
...though one may be overpowered, two can defend themselves.
A cord of three strands is not easily broken.

Ecclesiastes 4:9 & 12

We all love movies like the Book of Eli and the Mad Max series. One man, wandering the wasteland, surviving, and righting the wrongs that he comes across, for the good of all. What a great concept.

Those are movies. In real life, Eli would have been wiped out just as surely as K-Mart has been (in the movie, if you watch carefully, you'll see Eli's K-Mart name tag). Max Rockatansky would never have made it to Barter-Town or the Thunderdome. In a real world collapse, lone wolves will die.

We hear it all the time, "I'm going to just be on my own moving fast". Really? If that is your plan, do the rest of us a favor and send us the location of your gear caches, so that we can claim them when you die.

We are talking about a real world situation; you need a tribe. Set aside the action movie dreams, in a WROL situation, you won't even be able to sleep safely if you are alone.

You will need to identify like-minded individuals and organize them into a group and conduct training together. In this chapter, we're going to discuss who to seek out, who to avoid, and how best to organize your groups.

<u>Finding Like Minded People</u>

Most of us already have a group of friends who think like we do, that's why they are our friends. That's the first place we start; our own friends and family. Identify among your circle who is already concerned and begin discussing their thoughts about preparedness. You might already have allies.

Social media has become such an ingrained part of our lives that it's a great place to find others and share ideas. There are some serious cautions about making people you've met online part of your life-saving plans, however.

The only way to build lasting, trust-based relationships like the ones needed for preparedness is face-to-face interaction. If you join a preparedness group online, schedule a picnic-style meet-up so that you can actually meet people.

A large group setting is safer than meeting people one-on-one, and it will allow you to meet a number of people and start to make assessments. If you meet a few people that might fit with your group or yourself, gather contact information and then plan a smaller event with just those people. Eventually, you'll have a small group of dedicated folks that you've built a solid relationship with.

There is danger in selecting people online. First, there are legit crazy people out here who will get you into trouble if you affiliate yourself with them. Also, the minute you start talking about preparedness or exercising your rights (usually the same thing), the federal government will try and infiltrate your group. Fortunately, both of these types of people, the crazy and the Fed, act exactly the same.

Before I go further into this, let me cover a couple of important points:

1. People in law enforcement by and large are great people who care about their communities. However, ever since the 70s, US Federal law enforcement has sought to infiltrate and prosecute people who organize for preparedness or who are interested in their Constitutional rights.

2. "But we aren't breaking the law": That's absolutely true. And it's also absolutely true that the government does not care one bit. They like to keep tabs on what preparations you are making and why. First, if you develop large stashes of supplies and an emergency develops, they can label you as "hoarding" and seize your goods under the Defense Production Act. Second, as we've seen time and time again, the federal government inserts informants to try and convince your group to do something illegal. It's a hassle you'd rather not have.

3. "They only target bad people": Say what you want about Randy Weaver's personal beliefs, the courts have determined that he was entrapped by the ATF because their informant convinced him to break the law; he never considered it himself and in fact had refused to repeatedly.

I'm not being anti-government, I'm objectively analyzing risk. Understand that the risk exists and you'd rather not have to deal with it.

Anyone who you are considering for membership in your group who advocates taking action against the government, building explosives, or modifying weapons should be told clearly "NO" and that you desire absolutely no contact with them ever again.

If those people come back later, and try to contact you, then they are definitely trying to infiltrate your group and you should have nothing to do with them.

Our purpose is always survival, not any other goals. Don't let others talk you into anything else.

<u>Operational Security</u>

Once you've established a group, it's time for operational security, or OPSEC.

In our our modern society, so many tend to "narrate their lives" on social media for all to see. In the context of preparedness, this is a terrible thing.

You are creating target lists for bad actors or government agencies by posting all of your preparedness activity online. Your group should have a standing rule that no one posts about preparations. The first rule of Fight Club, as we all know, is to never talk about Fight Club.

In a crisis, desperate people will remember you posting your hidden stash of canned goods behind the dining room wall. They will at remember that you frequently mentioned being prepared.

Giving yourself a name is something a lot of groups do, and while I don't recommend it, there are some guidelines I'll give you, for the protection of your group.

- Groups with names are a red flag and WILL lead to government interest, even if it's just to find out what you are about. We want to avoid contact.

- The "M" word, MILITIA is dangerous. First, it attracts federal agents like unpaid taxes. Second, different cultures react to the word differently. For example, in Russia, "militia" are what the police are called and in the Middle East, it generally describes extremist groups.

- I would avoid anything even remotely military related as a name.

- A final caution about naming: The State of Michigan is using "gang membership" laws to prosecute militia people. The loose definition is a group with a name.

For security, avoid using social media platforms to organize or schedule. In the fine print, you'll see that even if you have a private group, you don't own the data, and they can shut down your group page anytime they want.

Conduct planning and organization via secure email or some type of secure messaging platform. Again, not because you're doing anything wrong, but because security matters and you don't want the hassle of unwanted attention.

Be careful who you talk to at work about preparedness, because you don't know how people will react now, pre-event, or post-event. Someone who seems supportive now, after 2 weeks have gone by without food or electricity, may eventually remember that you have a large supply of food.

For this reason, we apply OPSEC even more post-event. If you are the only person in the neighborhood not losing weight, the neighbors will wonder why. If everyone else is going hungry, and you're in the front yard preparing a feast from your stocks of food, someone will come by.

Here's where it gets a little harsh, but we have to remember our ultimate goal is our survival. Remember what we discussed in Chapter 2…"He who does not work does not eat". We don't just give out charity, we pay the hungry for their labor in food. We also don't allow them to move into our compound.

OPSEC is also why, in later volumes, we'll learn to train to conduct local security operations like checkpoints and patrols. Keeping people away so that they can't observe your location will keep them from being envious and doing bad things.

<u>Organizing Your Team</u>

Eventually, you will need to organize in some way. It's basic human nature and there will times when democracy won't work; a leader will be needed.

A good base-line for organizing is the US Special Forces Detachment Alpha model (A-Team). An A-Team consists of:

- Detachment Leader

- Assistant Detachment Leader

- Operations Chief

- Intelligence Chief

- 2 Communications Specialists

- 2 Medical Specialists

- 2 Engineering Specialists

- 2 Weapons Specialists

In the specialist realm, each one is cross-trained into another specialty. For example, one weapons specialist might also be a back-up medic, and one medic might also be a back-up communications person.

As you can see, it's a very adaptable team basis. In day-to-day operations, the communications and medical teams could report to the operations chief and the weapons and engineering specialists could report to the intelligence chief. When going out onto a patrol, you could make two teams, each led by one of the leaders, backed up by a section chief, and containing one specialist from each category.

Ideally, each of the 4 leadership roles would be specialists in one of the other areas.

How does a group of non-military people select a leader? Prior to the 1900s, for hundreds of years, military units elected their own leaders. This isn't a bad model, as long as there isn't a new election every time someone disagrees.

Some groups decide to have no leaders and no hierarchy, but that is a mistake. When a crisis happens, you can't have a group of people having a committee meeting to decide what to do.

There are other organizations that work well with other groups, such as the US Army Squad (one squad leader and 2 fire teams of 4, 9 total) or the USMC Squad (one squad leader and 3 fire teams of 4, 13 total), but those are predominantly just for ground infantry or patrolling operations.

The key is to decide on what specialties you need, appoint people to fill them, and decide on leadership.

The following are some suggested specialties to seek out for your group:

- Medical: We are seeking at least Paramedic/EMT level, and it would be best to have a nurse or doctor.

- Communications: No matter what you think you will be doing after a WROL situation, you will need to communicate with others, even if it's just listening for news. For this role, a licensed Amateur Radio Operator would be best.

- Engineering: This is more than what we traditionally call engineers. We are thinking more like a combat engineer. One who can build what needs to be built, fix what ever is broken, and the like. Agriculture would be included here.

- Weapons: Although we're using the US Military team term, we aren't looking for guys who can operate obscure weapons, we mean security specialists who could also form a hunting party, or build defenses, maybe investigators who could go out and gather information, or just trained people to protect the others. Make no mistake, everyone is responsible for security, but a few dedicated security specialists will help.

- Planning/Operations: You'll need people who are good at planning, inventorying supplies, analyzing stock levels, etc. These people will help decide what needs to be done to improve your food or supply stocks. Pre-Event, they help others plan for their own stocks and communal group stocks, and post-event they help decide what needs to be done.

These are the basic areas we need covered. You could create all kinds of sub-teams, if you had the manpower.

Remember: Everyone will be involved in the defense of the group, not just the security team. The security or weapons team should be specialists who possess skills beyond just trigger pulling. Things like small unit tactics and patrolling are far more skill-intensive than you might think.

<u>Adding People to the Group</u>

After you've organized and assigned people to their sections, you may later have someone approach about joining your group.

Remember all of the discussion above about vetting, but also consider how well a new person might fit with the group. Things to consider are personality, how well they might get along, whether already have their own supplies, and whether they have an exceptional skill you might need.

As an example, a doctor or skilled radio operator would be a serious asset, but a web developer might not be helpful unless they had some other skills.

Before making a final decision, have several other group members spend some time with them, and maybe invite them in as a probationary member, until the team decides if they are a good fit.

Post-Event, in a true WROL situation, we would almost never add a new person to our group. They would have to bring an exceptional skill set and their own gear for us to accept another mouth to feed and person to house. Infiltration by bad actors will be a real threat.

<u>Base Line Standard</u>

- Identify and fully vet all potential team members

- Organize the team in some way

- Conduct Operational Security training and set OPSEC standards for group membership

- Assign roles and appoint leaders

- Establish guidelines for adding new members

Chapter 11

Communication Minimum Standard

He who answers before listening,
That is his folly & his shame

Proverbs 18:13

Knowing what is happening around you and having the ability to communicate with your family or group is going to become vital in a WROL situation. Without normal communications and news channels like cell phones, radios, and the internet, rumors and panic will spread far faster than facts and reason.

We learned this at the beginning of the COVID 19 pandemic in 2020. As lockdowns began, it seemed that everyone had a cousin or a friend at the FBI or DHS announcing that roadblocks and checkpoints were going up, but those things never materialized. Fortunately, traditional communications channels were up, and that kept the panic in check with factual information.

But what if it hadn't been? People would have gotten panicked, and lashed out. You need to plan for this and develop a few bare minimum methods for gathering and sharing information. A lot of people focus on communications gear for sharing, but we're going to get into gear for gathering information passively as well.

The Tactical Wisdom verse at the top of the page should be your guiding principle here. Spreading information before confirming it, leads to folly and eventual shame. We are going to develop here first the ability to listen for news and information, then develop our capability to share information with our teams.

Let's set a couple of ground rules here first.

We are talking about communications in WROL situation. In other words, law and order is non-existent. The reason I say this is because I know that some Amateur Radio licensee is going to give this book a bad review because I discuss broadcasting outside legal FCC limits. In a WROL situation, the FCC is the least of my worries.

The second ground rule about our discussion of radio equipment for WROL is use that in a WROL situation, you have to agree that a lot of the "nuisance traffic" people are worried about and use as reasons not to use particular radio systems or frequencies will go away. There won't be local businesses using the MURS frequencies, there won't be neighborhood kids on the FRS channels playing, and there won't even be interstate truckers on the CB frequencies (even though they are an OUTSTANDING source of intelligence, but we'll get to that in a bit).

Lastly, for the purposes of the Base Line Training Manual, remember that we are talking about minimum standards, and a base line. We are not going to get into digital modes, sending data over HF, or anything that advanced. We're going to discuss gathering from long-distance sources, and short-to-medium range voice communications for your team. Those are the bare minimum.

Information Gathering

All day, every day, information is being shared all over the world, and all you need to tap into that intelligence information goldmine is an antenna and a tuner.

"Shortwave" radio, also known as "High Frequency" or "HF", has been used to share information and news for about 100 years. The actual frequencies used range from the medium-wave (where modern AM radio is) though the HF band, with most activity in the 3-30 MHZ range (HF).

We're not going to get into a technical discussion here, but amateur radio sites are a great way to learn about the science of it, if you need to. For our discussion, we just are going to discuss the equipment you need and how to best use it.

In disasters, Amateur Radio operators around the world broadcast news and pass on information via radio. For our purposes, we need the ability to receive information from this band, so that we can hear first-hand reports from long distances to gather a "big picture" of what is happening. It will enable us to counter rumors and understand what is happening around us.

It will also enable us to learn about threats that may be coming our way in the future. For example, if you know in advance, from the information here, about an amateur station a hundred miles away, you can monitor their traffic and learn what is happening there, which may impact you soon.

With this in mind, you need to develop a capability to RECEIVE shortwave radio, with a Single-Side Band (SSB) capability. You can buy radios that receive these transmissions and keep them charged and ready to go.

The features you need on a shortwave receiver are:

- FM/MW/SW - FM radio, Medium Wave, Shortwave. You need to be able to receive all three bands.

- SSB - You need a receiver capable of receiving Single Side Band.

- Scan Feature - The radio should have the ability to either scan all bands, or to scan the frequencies you program.

- Antenna - While stock antennas are good, you need to buy additional long wire antennas for this particular application, to increase the range at which you can receive.

Once you get a receiver with these qualities, you'll be amazed at the distance at which you receive broadcasts.

A quality radio with these features generally runs about $100-$200, but it's money well spent, because in a WROL situation, information is priceless, and you won't be able to buy one at any price. Get one now and learn how to use it.

If you choose to get an amateur license, you can go ahead get a transceiver in this frequency range, but they are expensive, and for our purposes, listening is good enough.

You can find amateur radio broadcast frequencies near you with a quick online search, and you should develop that list NOW, and create a list that you can print out and have available.

Many emergency organizations will be broadcasting emergency information in these bands, such as the Red Cross, FEMA, and the Salvation Army. Use the scan feature to find active channels.

In a WROL situation, use a notebook (again, paper/pencils are overlooked preparedness items) to write down information received. Sometimes, patterns and usefulness of information only becomes apparent over time, so documentation is the key to long-term analysis.

Scanners are another good tool to monitor local police, fire, and emergency agencies. You need a scanner capable of receiving your local and state agencies, so do some research ahead of time. Most agencies are now using digital systems, so you'll need a "trunk tracker" type of scanner.

Do some research and find out the local "failsafe" or "fallback" frequencies. If grid power goes down, the digital systems may not have enough power to be sustainable. The local agencies may fall back to older VHF/UHF frequencies.

Don't overlook programming your scanner to receive all FRS/GMRS/MURS frequencies (discussed below) because then you will be able to detect people using short range radios near your location. This is VITAL because if you detect people approaching you using radios, you may be in extreme danger, and listening in on their communications can help you determine their intentions.

Even in a pre-event situation, this can help. I once was able to monitor an armed ANTIFA security team that was following me to try and get my license plate number. If I hadn't been listening in, I would never have known. Listening in also allowed me to evade them, and I only went back to my car after hearing them discussing that they had no idea where I went. Develop this capability, because they are using the same systems we're going to discuss.

CB Radio

CB Radio was popular in the 70s and 80s, and used to require a license. Now, it's only used by truckers, generally on Channel 19, and no license is required.

CB is a good preparedness radio system for road movement and rural use.

First, since it's mostly fallen out of favor, other than on Channel 19, those channels are available for our use right now, with no license required. CB has 40 channels, and if you add in SSB capability,

you have 120 possible "channels" to use. Before I get another
negative comment from an Amateur Radio Operator, it's still only
40 channels, but 120 communication options.

CB operates in the HF band, and is currently limited to 4 watts of
power on standard channels and 12 watts on SSB. They will
generally get you about 3-20 miles of range, depending on the
terrain. Handheld units get less range, due to antenna height.
SSB channels get longer range, and are capable of very long
range communications in certain atmospheric conditions,

CB Radio can be a great way to gather information both pre and
post event. Listening now to Channel 19, you'll hear about
information impacting travel on the highways, as truckers share
information with each other.

Post-event, there may still be some limited commerce going on
and listening in may provide information on conditions elsewhere.

For our use, a vehicle convoy could operate using CB channels for
vehicle-to-vehicle communions, and VHF/UHF for interpersonal
communications. In other words, each vehicle could have a CB
mounted, and each person in the vehicle has a personal radio on a
different frequency for use when out of the vehicle.

If you sent a dismount team ahead to scout out a bridge, or
danger area, those on foot could communicate with each other on
their personal radios, but communicate back to the vehicles with a
handheld CB they took with them. This frees up channels for each
element to talk to their own element.

FRS/GMRS Radios

The Family Radio Service (FRS) and General Mobile Radio Service
(GMRS) are the common blister-pack radios you can buy at
Walmart/Target and they are widely available and widely in use.
These radios operate in the UHF band and are very susceptible to

obstructions, so the range is generally 1-2 miles for handhelds, and about 5 miles for vehicle mounted radios.

Under FCC regulations, the FRS is limited to 0.5 Watts, and the GMRS has varying limits from 0.5 Watts on the channels shared with FRS, to 5 Watts on the lower channels, and 50 Watts on the higher ones. FRS does not require a license, but GMRS does. In a WROL situation, none of that will matter, but I'm providing it anyway.

Additionally, it's with noting that you cannot currently, pre-event BROADCAST in the FRS frequencies or GMRS frequencies with any radio that has a removable antenna and can be programmed from the front panel. Those are FCC rules, and they don't matter one bit in a WROL situation.

These radio frequencies are perfect for short-range team communications. For example, for day-to-day use around your location, communication between team members on a patrol, and communications from an observation post back to your location.

Keep in mind these are for SHORT-RANGE communications.

FCC regulations aside, if you are going to use these frequencies post-event, in a WROL situation with no regard for the FCC, don't buy the ones in the blister pack. Buy a UHF band amateur radio and program these frequencies in. As a side note, the FCC rules don't apply if you are only listening.

As a reminder, under FCC rules, anyone can transmit at any power level on any frequency in an emergency.

<u>MURS Radios</u>

MURS is the Multi-Use Radio Service. It does not require a license. Under FCC Rules, power is limited to 2 Watts (again, in WROL we won't worry about power restrictions). As it operates in

VHF, a little better range is given. You can expect 2-3 miles with a handheld unit and around 10 with an externally mounted antenna or roll-up antenna.

Locally, I hear the local Walmart at about 4 miles regularly, in urban terrain, on a hand-held.

MURS radios are designed for personal or business use and could be used pre-event for whatever purpose you want, as long as you aren't serving a foreign nation. They are my default radio frequencies of choice.

Many in the preparedness community scoff at this recommendation, saying that there are too many businesses on it. I challenge that on day 6 of a WROL situation, I'm not going to get much interference from people stocking shelves anywhere.

<u>Ok, Now What?</u>

So now that we've looked at all these systems, what do we do? What do we choose?

The key is to DIVERSIFY.

You need to establish, before a WROL situation, your group's "Signal Operating Instructions". This is your radio plan, such as what frequencies to use and when, and when to make contact, etc.

Once you develop this plan, everyone should have a copy for reference and have it with them at all times.

The best solution is a mix of all these radio systems. Determine what frequencies your group will use for what types of situations, are write that down. The reason for writing it down is that you want to be able to call all your channels by a team common name, rather than it's FCC name. For example, if someone is listening, and you say, "OK, everyone switch to FRS 6", the opposition knows where to go to listen in.

As an example, a team may decide on a mix of FRS/GMRS channels for day to day operations. They don't call them by their FCC name. Let's say that their main channel is FRS 5, rather than calling it "FRS 5", they say "MAIN". Their security post channel is GMRS 14, but they call it "TAC 1". Only your team will know what channels you are using.

If you have a large team that will all be working together, you need to establish a "MAIN" channel for everyone to be able to put out an emergency message or information for the whole group, and then designate alternate channels for each sub group.

Using our vehicle movement example from above, every one could monitoring the main channel, but every one in Vehicle 1 could use FRS 6, Vehicle 2 FRS 4, etc. This will allow your teams to talk to each other in their own teams, while still being able to communicate among the teams.

You could apply this across a compound as well. Everyone could monitor the main channel, the farming/agriculture team on it's own channel, security team on another, medical on yet another.

The key is to have equipment with the capability to monitor more than a single channel. Radios like the Baofeng's that are so popular have a "dual-watch" capability to monitor 2 channels at once, and this is a good feature. Scan features are good too, but having a transceiver scan isn't as fast as a dedicated scanner, and it causes batteries to drain fast.

There are many handhelds with a dual watch capability, so pick one that has it. There are also vehicle mounted or base station radios that have "quad-watch", and they're a good thing to have as well.

They key to all of this is to have a written communications plan that EVERYONE knows.

A great resource for this is American Redoubt Radio Operators Network (AMRRON). If you join their network, they give you a pre-written set of Signal Operating Instructions, including security authentication protocols, that you could adopt for your group with minimal changes.

<u>Channel 3 Project</u>

That's all great, but how do we find others?   Or, if we are moving through an area, how can we reach to other preparedness-minded people for information on local issues or perhaps a night's rest in a dry location?

The American Redoubt Radio Operators Network came through again, and this one doesn't require membership. They established the Channel 3 protocol that has pretty much become standard throughout the preparedness community.

This plan calls for people to call out on or monitor the most commonly-used license free frequencies at certain times.

- Set your radio to one of these: CB-3, FRS-3, or MURS-3.

- Listen or call from 2 minutes before the hour to 2 minutes after the hour.

- Every hour.

- Under this protocol, you could reach preparedness minded people for information or assistance anywhere.

Make the Channel 3 Project part of your Communication Plan and if you have a fixed base (meaning you aren't moving), monitor the channel as often as you can.

<u>Sample Basic Plan</u>

A good general outline to follow is:

- CB channel for vehicle movement/convoys

- FRS/GMRS channels (4 or 5 different ones) for everyday tasks/team communications

- MURS channel used for patrol-to-base reporting or OP-to-base reporting, because of the slightly longer range (You could use CB as well, if outside of an urban area)

- Monitoring of the Channel 3 Project, while NOT USING the channel 3's for any other use. Keep those channels free.

<u>Communications Security</u>

Communications Security (COMSEC) is a huge topic, and here we are just going to cover the basics.

First, many in the preparedness community have a misconception about the ability to stop the US government from listening in on your communications. Let's be clear: The government of the United States is not going to let you buy any equipment that they can't monitor. It's just a fact. So, first understand that your can't buy an un-crackable radio.

Second, you most likely aren't going to be dealing with nation-state level intercept capability. What I mean is that, despite what all the YouTube radio commandos tell you, you aren't important enough for China, Russia, the US, or the UN to monitor, track, and destroy. This isn't a movie and we aren't a group of high school kids fighting off the Russian/South American invasion of Calumet, shouting "Wolverines" every chance we get.

In all honesty, if you are just trying to survive, no one will be trying to monitor you, because they don't know where you are and you aren't actively causing anyone trouble. There are techniques for if you are, but that's a topic for farther along our training manual series.

So, for our purposes, the first COMSEC technique is what we discussed above…assigning different names to channels so that if anyone does happen across your broadcasts, they won't know what other channels you are using. Yes, they could scan, but are they going to go to the trouble?

Principle two is never using real names on the radio. Someone listening in could get a name, and then try to talk their way into the community by claiming to know that name or use it in some other community ("I know Thomas over on Pine Bluff Rd"). Everyone should have a callsign.

Next, understand that we talking about short-range radio communications. You may well be talking to other places at long range about news and information, but the communications you want to protect are your short-range tactical communications, like security or foraging parties. In order for someone to monitor them, they have to be relatively close to you. Aggressive security patrolling and "satellite patrolling" of likely monitoring locations, like a high hill, would reduce the ability for someone to monitor your local communications without detection.

Authentication, such as daily network passwords, should be used so that someone on the radio can be verified. Passwords between neighboring groups should also be devised. These should never be given out via radio, and changed once used over the air. The AMRRON reference above includes a great way to authenticate other preparedness groups, operating from the same AMRRON set of instructions.

While the use of deceptive codes is against FCC regulations, as long as the purpose is not to deceive, codes can be used. For example, the ARRL has a complete set of codes that they use on the air. Establish names for locations and people, rather than their actual names.

Establish a standing procedure that if an un-authenticated voice tries to make contact on your frequency, that all units know to automatically and immediately switch to a pre-planned alternate frequency. Everyone should do this without communicating the fact on the compromised channel.

<u>Pro-words</u>

Pro-words are standard words used on US military networks to clarify and speed up communications. A few standard pro-words should be known by everyone in your group. These are also standards on the AMRRON Channel 3 Project.

- ALL AFTER: I am referring to everything after...

- ALL BEFORE: I am referring to everything before...

- BREAK: I am separating into a second message. Can also be used in an emergency to break in to a conversation.

- CORRECTION: An error has been made, corrected information follows.

- I SAY AGAIN: I am repeating.

- I SPELL: Phonetic spelling follows.

- OUT: This is the end of my transmission; no response needed.

- OVER: This is the end of my transmission; waiting for you to respond (NOTE: you will never say "over and out", as they have opposite meanings).

- RELAY TO: Please forward this message to…

- SAY AGAIN: Please repeat your last transmission.

- TIME: What follows is the time of the report/ observation.

- WAIT: Pausing for a few seconds.

- WAIT OUT: Pausing for more than a few seconds.

- WRONG: Your last transmission was incorrect, corrected version is…

These are by no means all of the Pro-Words, but these are sufficient to begin communications. Your team could also learn American Radio Relay League "Q-codes" or similar to speed up reporting.

<u>NATO Phonetic Alphabet</u>

For clarity, learn to use the NATO Phonetic Alphabet.

A	**A**lfa/Alpha	AL FAH
B	**B**ravo	BRAH VOH
C	**C**harlie	CHAR LEE
D	**D**elta	DELL TAH
E	**E**cho	ECK OH
F	**F**oxtrot	FOKS TROT
G	**G**olf	GOLF
H	**H**otel	HOH TELL
I	**I**ndia	IN DEE AH
J	**J**uliett	JEW LEE ETT
K	**K**ilo	KEY LOH
L	**L**ima	LEE MAH
M	**M**ike	MIKE
N	**N**ovember	NO VEMBER
O	**O**scar	OSS CAH

P	**P**apa	PAH PAH
Q	**Q**uebec	KEH BECK
R	**R**omeo	ROW ME OH
S	**S**ierra	SEE AIRRAH
T	**T**ango	TANG OH
U	**U**niform	YOU NEE FORM
V	**V**ictor	VIK TAH
W	**W**hiskey	WISS KEY
X	**X**-ray	ECKS RAY
Y	**Y**ankee	YANG KEY
Z	**Z**ulu	ZOO LOO

Maintaining Readiness

The biggest problem in Communications Preparedness is the tendency to not be actually ready.

We tend to buy the gear, get it programmed, charge it up, and then store it away.

One of the very first indicators of most emergencies will be the loss of the existing communications network, and, in the event the network is still up and running, it will be severely overloaded.

In other words, right from the outset of most emergencies, you won't be able to communicate via traditional methods.

What this means for us is that we need to keep our radios with us, at least available, throughout our days. This is easy for those of us who use radios in our day jobs, but for the rest of us, it presents a challenge.

If you buy a small enough hand-held, it can be kept in your EDC gear and therefore available, as long as you make sure to charge it regularly and bring along a way to charge it.

For a larger vehicle-type radio, the unit and it's antenna could just be kept stored in the trunk, only to be taken out if you need it. The unit could also be kept under a seat.

A great idea for vehicle radios or CB's is to mount it on the back of a wooden clipboard. This way, it can be stored in the trunk, and to mount it, you just slide the bottom of the clipboard down between the seats and the radio is mounted, standing upright. The clip part could hold your channel listing or authentication codes.

<u>Pre-Event Testing</u>

As you are developing your communications plan, monitor the channels you plan on using before committing to them. If you notice that a group of neighborhood kids are messing around on FRS-4, don't use that channel. I know earlier I said that the kids won't be playing on them, but the adults might be using them, and unless they are in your group, you don't know their intentions.

Test and monitor all of your planned frequencies and you could also test ranges with other members of your group.

Research

Do some online research and learn what local amateur radio frequencies and repeaters are in use in your area. In an emergency, monitoring them can provide you with valuable intelligence information as the amateur radio people discuss what's happening around them. You should monitor them regularly.

Similarly, learn the local amateur radio emergency frequencies like SkyWarn and ARES (Amateur Radio Emergency Service) channels. These will be invaluable in a WROL situation to learn what is going locally, to include what local government is doing as far as traffic control, road closures, evacuations, etc.

You don't have to be licensed to monitor.

Also, these groups all hold weekly or biweekly training networks. These are great to listen in on for training purposes and to gather information.

Licensing

Getting an amateur radio license can open up an entire world of communications and a great hobby, with tons of learning potential. I recommend at least one person in your group, preferably your communications specialist, get a license.

Whether or not to get licensed yourself is a decision you all have to make for yourselves.

I personally have not, although I interact with a lot of great people who have. I personally just decided that I didn't want to invite more government oversight into my life and I'm not willing to agree to allow a federal agent access to "inspect my equipment without delay" whenever they want.

My other concern is the Defense Production Act, which allows the government to seize any known equipment or supplies that the local FEMA administrator decides that he needs. If I'm not on the "approved high-power radio list", they can't come looking for my gear.

It's a great hobby full of great people (and more than a few "Karen's"), but each of us must make our own choice.

<u>Base Line Minimum Standard</u>

- Handheld VHF/UHF radio, programmable, with Dual Watch

- Some type of earpiece/microphone combination, allowing silent radio listening

- FM/MW/SW Receiver with SSB Capability and long wire antenna

- CB Radio for vehicle use (preferably with SSB capability)

- Consider additional handheld CB radio

- Written Communication Plan

<u>Resources</u>

1. American Redoubt Radio Operators Network: www.amrron.com

2. American Radio Relay League: www.arrl.org

Tactical Wisdom

Base Line Training Manual

Chapter 12

Functional Fitness for Preparedness

She dresses herself with strength
And makes her arms strong.

Proverbs 31:17

After stocking a first aid it, getting ourselves into shape is the next best thing we can do for preparedness. No matter who you are, there is something you can do to improve yourself in fitness, with just a few minutes a day.

The more physically fit you are, the more resistant you are to illness and physical injury. This is proven scientific fact, and it's also proven that doing literally ANYTHING physical can help improve your fitness.

We're going to discuss a few specific ideas to improve our fitness, because let's face it, we can all use a little more of it, but I'm in no means an expert. Find someone who is and get some solid advice.

In our Resource section at the end of this chapter, you'll find the website of my fitness guru, Drew Baye. His Project Kratos: Harder to Kill program is a great resource. I quote Drew regularly, and he often says "Do something every day to make yourself harder to kill". That philosophy is the basis of this chapter.

For our purposes, we are only discussing FUNCTIONAL fitness, which means strengthening those areas and improving in those areas with a direct impact on preparedness or combat skills. There is certainly a benefit to being able to train for a 10-K or a marathon, but that is NOT our goal. Our goal is straightening in specific movements that have direct applications.

Let's please the lawyers first: Before beginning any exercise program, consult with a doctor. Nothing in this chapter is to be construed as medical advice.

Before we begin, I know a lot of you may skip this chapter, or say "but I'm in such bad shape, I can't improve". Understand that everyone started somewhere and these ideas will cost you nothing. If you're already in shape, still read on. I've seen "gym fit" guys collapse in a 3 mile ruck.   People who run every day, can't necessarily throw a solid punch. Give it a try, and even if you take small steps to start, do something every single day to improve.

First, understand that doing literally anything is an improvement over doing nothing. If we begin with that small step in mind, we can build from there.

<u>The First Step - Literally</u>

The first step in functional fitness is to understand that in a WROL situation, the ability to WALK is the first physical skill we need. This may seem simple, because we all walk every day. The difference is the ability to walk a long distance at one time.

In any WROL situation, vehicles will either have limited fuel available, or will be totally unavailable. Learning to walk distances in one stretch is our first step.

Even if we have vehicles available, there are many places we'll
need to look at or go that a vehicle would hinder, for example,
gathering wild plants, hunting, or patrolling for our local security.

So, the first fitness goal we should have is conditioning our body,
and especially our feet, to walk long distances without stopping.
We're not worried about speed, just distance. You'll be surprised
how quickly our feet and lower shins get used to only walking
short distances at one time.

Begin walking today, and gradually increase the distances that you
walk.

Yes, you can literally walk off weight.

<u>Flexibility</u>

We need to improve our flexibility. Just working out in general
does not improve flexibility, only stretching does that.

You can start with Yoga, or some other type of stretching, but
consider the range of movement we may need in preparedness to
keep yourself on track.

We need the ability to reach over our head and down to the
ground. That may seem overly simplistic, but when was the last
time you tried both of those? Ever dropped a pen and almost fell
over trying to get it?

Work on developing flexibility in all directions through stretching:
Reaching, bending, twisting.

Working on joint flexibility also reduces the impact of joint locks
and pain compliance techniques that others may try on you.

<u>Combatives Training</u>

Our primary source of cardio training should come from some type of "combative training", whether it be a traditional martial art, self defense, Krav Maga, or something similar.

Martial arts training develops a martial mindset, the will to win, self-confidence, and basic fighting spirit, while improving flexibility, mobility, balance, and cardiovascular fitness.

Here, the particular style is not nearly as important as just doing something.   Lots of people ask, "Which art is best for me to start?", but the fact is that if you are starting out with no training, literally anything is better than nothing.

All martial arts training, if we are honest, gets you moving, your heart pumping, teaches you the mechanics of striking, and develops defensive skill.

The only danger is getting into purely sport or dance styles.

Invest some time in researching the school you want to join. Meet with the instructor and talk about philosophy, and explain to them your goals. Observe a few classes.

Avoid "McDojo" schools that are really just belt factories, designed to take as much of your money as possible, as quickly as they can. These are easy to spot: Ask to observe a black belt level class and if there are people under 10 years old in it, with sloppy movements, then don't sign up.

Avoid unrealistic styles that are almost entirely kicking (we're looking at you Tae Kwon Do), as it's not applicable to a WROL situation. You won't be moving around in marital arts uniform pants, and wearing a sidearm or other gear limits your ability to kick high.

While you should indeed develop ground fighting skills, avoid any art that focuses entirely on ground fighting. While it's acceptable for self-defense in the current environment (if attacked by one person), if attacked in a WROL situation, you don't want to be wrestling around on the ground, while his friends steal your stuff and stab you.

Pick something well-rounded. Don't limit yourself to one style. While I teach Tang Soo Do (a Korean Martial Art), I also study & teach Krav Maga, have studied & teach ground fighting skills from Brazilian Jiu Jitsu, and study Filipino stick and blade fighting.

When training in traditional martial arts, there is often a focus on ceremony and beginning from unrealistic, traditional stances. Once you've learned them in that way, start practicing them from a fighting stance that you are likely to use in real life, so that the skill has real world potential for you.

The same goes for traditional martial arts "forms" training. These may be called Kata in Japanese arts, or Hyung/Poomsae in Korean arts, but the idea is the same: A prearranged series of movements tied together in a pattern. Once you learn a form, pull out the combative combinations that you will use together in real life and train on them from a realistic stance.

Begin training in some type of self-defense, to develop a fighting spirit, self-confidence, and basic defensive skills, while improving your cardiovascular fitness.

Strength and Balance/Bodyweight Training

We should develop both upper and lower body muscular strength, while focusing on exercises that apply to motions we may need. That sounds complex, but it really isn't. The exercise you do should have some direct application to physical skills you'll need in a WROL situation.

For example, the ability to get quickly down on the ground and to quickly get back up are both skills you need, right? What exercises contribute directly to improving our ability to do this? Easy, burpees are nothing more than doing these two things together.

While patrolling or moving, you will frequently need to "take a knee". Either just to observe, or to assume a firing position. Lunges are this exact motion.

Even the old-school daily staple of push-ups, sit-ups, and squats work on functional fitness.

1. Pushups: Punching/getting up from the ground

2. Sit Ups: Getting up from the ground after a fall

3. Squats: Getting down low/moving through low passages/getting into cover

When I was a young man, I couldn't figure out why the drill instructors made us do bear walks, crab walks, and duck walks, but a few weeks later I learned that these exercises were designed to improve my ability to move while behind cover, because they use muscle groups that we normally neglect in our daily lives.

Things like this are what I mean by improving our "functional fitness". Our modern, tech-driven lives have caused us to neglect certain muscle groups. Even when we "go to the gym", we work on things that improve our appearance, but not necessarily our functional fitness. That's not to say there is no benefit, just not a preparedness benefit.

When we suddenly find ourselves in a WROL situation is not the time to figure out that we've neglected certain areas.

The following exercises will help, but by no means am I a fitness expert. I certainly recommend developing your own program.
This is not an exhaustive list, they are just a few exercises that will help with functional fitness.

- Push-Ups: Upper body strength/punching/pushing/ getting up

- Squats: Ability to lower yourself or to get up

- Sit-Ups: Getting up from prone/core strength

- Burpees: The ability to get down quickly and to get up quickly

- Lunges: Getting into and out of the kneeling position

- Trunk Twists: Ability to generate power when punching

- Crab Walk: Movement behind cover

- Bear Walk: Movement behind cover

- Duck Walk: Movement behind cover

As you can see, just starting out by doing a few these each day can help start you on the path to functional fitness for survival.

The basic combat movement technique of the low crawl is excellent exercise and when you try it for the first time over any distance, you'll learn that you need to develop those specific muscles.

Rucking

Probably the common physical motion you'll do in a WROL situation is walking carrying a backpack. We call that "Rucking", and the best way to develop your body to be able to do it well is to just get out and do it now.

But first, let's differentiate this from some of the "Rucking" sporting events you see. Those events generally use a weight in the backpack, which doesn't actually simulate carrying a load, because the weight is all concentrated in one place. They also do their events for time, focusing on speed while carrying the load.

Since we're preparing to do this for survival, we aren't concerned at all with time. We are concerned with distance.

We also want to practice carrying our actual Get Home Bag, Patrol Bag, or Full Ruck. In fact, that's the training progression we'll use, since those bags start lighter, and then get heavier.

To begin rucking, start off with walking every day for a week first, if you aren't very physically active. Once you've gotten your feet and shins acclimated to walking, then we will begin rucking.

Start off with your lightest bag, most likely the Get Home Bag. Carry it with the real items in it, so that it's the actual weight. To begin, you could start without water, which is heavy, and then add it in later.

Put the pack on and just start walking. Don't worry about trying to do a 15 minute mile, like rucking videos tell you to, you aren't a light infantry fighter rushing to get in position before an enemy force is ready. We are just training to be able to move carrying a load. For the Get Home Bag, I'd practice walking in urban terrain, or whatever environment you usually commute on. For this, sidewalks and streets are fine, and if it's safe, maybe an alley or two.

Start with just a couple of miles and then work your way up to whatever your normal commute is. While we aren't concerned with speed at first, you'll find that the more you train, the faster you'll go. Just don't worry about trying to get faster.

Once you've mastered movement with the Get Home Bag, move to our EDC/Patrol Bag that we discussed earlier. It's probably a bit heavier than the get home bag. We're going to change a couple of things up here, to remain realistic.

First, find a wooded area to train in. Even in urban areas, you can find wooded trail areas to train in. If you just absolutely can't (maybe you live in NYC or Chicago), don't worry about it, but it's preferred. You'll begin walking on the trails for the first few times, but then move to rucking cross-country, because you will want to avoid trails in a WROL situation, and it's harder to move cross-country.

Next, carry something in your hands. If you live in a rural area, go ahead and carry a long firearm, if that's what you'll be carrying in a WROL situation and it won't cause you issues. For those in an urban areas, carrying a metal (for weight) walking stick in both hands simulates carrying a rifle. The reason for this is that in a WROL situation, you won't be able to use your hands to negotiate obstacles, or at least one hand. This trains you to consider how to negotiate obstacles with either one hand or no hands to assist.

You'll also notice that even carrying a very light object while walking leads to soreness in your arms. That's progress and we're training our body to survive.

Next, add in wearing your belt kit as well.

Once we've gotten to where we can move safely cross-country, start trying to move quietly wearing the pack cross-country. Moving quietly is what we'll be doing in a real-life situation.

Remember, we aren't just hiking. We are training to survive and move in a WROL situation, so we're not just mechanically covering ground. We're moving, observing, and trying to avoid being seen or heard.

When you are training in cross country rucking, train also for security halts. If you stop to rest, don't just sit down on a log and chill. Find a covered and concealed location, set your ruck down as either a weapons rest or a back rest, and rest tactically. As a side benefit, you'll see a lot more nature this way too.

Once you've gotten pretty comfortable with the EDC/Patrol Pack, move to your full ruck. After that, your full ruck with your EDC/Patrol pack attached. Everything is a training progression.

As a side note, spend some time training on taking off and putting on your various packs silently.

<u>Recap</u>

In order to improve our ability to survive in a WROL scenario, we all need to improve our functional fitness. Taking a few minutes a day will help build progress incrementally.

Don't worry about be a marathon runner on day one, just get up and do something.

We all need some sort of self-defense or martial arts training to develop our cardio training, to build self-confidence, and to develop the warrior spirit.

Some type of physical fitness and strength training should be done by everyone, even if it starts out minor. Fitness is preparedness.

The best real-world training we can do on a regular basis is rucking, since foot movement carrying a load is what we'll do most often.

<u>Base Line Standard:</u>

- Train in some type of self-defense or martial arts at least one day a week, even if it's solo training.

- Conduct strength training, even if it's just bodyweight calisthenics, 3-4 days a week.

- Train by rucking (or walking) 2-3 days per week.

<u>Resources:</u>

Strength Training:

Project Kratos, Harder to Kill Program; www.baye.com

Base Line Training Manual

Chapter 13

Specialized Preparedness Tools

*If the axe is dull & it's edge unsharpened,
More strength is needed, but skill will bring success.*

Ecclesiates 10:10

We began with a discussion that skills are more important than gear, but there are a few specialized items that will improve your ability to survive that we should discuss. I won't get into specific brands or sources, but we will discuss features and functions that you should look for when making your own decisions.

Remember though, that you may very well have to carry everything that you buy, so keep weight & portability in mind.

Electricity will also be an issue. While you may very well have a generator or solar panels, we don't want to unnecessarily tax our systems with cool gadgets and battery charging for everything we own. That being said, some things, like lighting and night vision, will require it.

<u>Shovel</u>

In a WROL world, digging will be a common task. You will need to dig observation posts, defensive positions, fire pits, trash pits, and sanitation holes.

For the purposes of the Base Line standard, every member of your group needs to have some type of collapsible shovel. There are many manufacturers and most are well made. A good idea is to start with one that meets US military standards. Millions of dollars go into the research and adoption of military gear, and this way you'll know that it meets rigorous use standards.

When buying a collapsible shovel, buy also a method for carrying it. Again, US military surplus meets this standard.   A US government issue shovel case will be made to attach to a backpack/ruck/belt. You could also buy a shovel that fits into one of these holders, even if it's not the originally intended one.

A key feature to look for in any collapsible shovel is the ability to lock it open at 90 degrees, to allow you to use it as a hoe or an improvised weapon.

Another good option is one of the shovels you can find on the Internet that has handle sections that screw together. Inside these sections, there are usually other tool heads, like a knife blade, a saw blade, etc. These come with a shovel head that does lock open at 90 degrees, and generally come with one edge of the shovel sharpened for use as a axe. They come in varying lengths and with extra features. The one I personally choose has a fire steel and a whistle in the cap as well. Shop around and pick what's best for you.

As a supplement, not a replacement, a small hand shovel, like a garden trowel, can be added just for use for sanitation, but only after you've added a regular collapsible shovel of some type to your gear.

<u>Axe</u>

You will need some type of camp axe/hatchet for use around a camp site. We're not talking about a full size timber axe, but one for camp-related or survival-related tasks, even for cutting your way out of a blocked door.

First, it's important to differentiate fighting tomahawks from a hand axe. They are NOT the same thing. While a tomahawk could be used to cut wood, that's not it's true purpose and could dull the blade so that it's not ready for it's primary use. Hand axes are IN ADDITION to any fighting axes. For purposes of the Base Line Training Manual, we won't get into fighting tomahawks, as they aren't a bare necessity. Besides, do you really envision getting into an action-movie tomahawk duel? The French & Indian War is over.

You can buy a small, hand-type axe that can be either attached to your pack or stored inside it. Buy a good name brand and only use as designed.

The only real feature it needs is an axe blade on one side and a hammer face on the other.   It also needs some type of a case that covers the blade for safe carriage. A cover that has the capability to attach to your pack is a good plus.

You can also find axes just like the shovel we discussed above. I found one that has an axe head, with a flat hammer face on the other side, but the screw-together handles also contain a knife and saw blade, screwdriver tips, a whistle, a compass, and a fire steel. I was fortunate enough that the one I found had a reducer that will allow me to attach the axe handle to the shovel handle, enabling me to make a full sized axe. Shop around for the best tool and read reviews.

<u>Lighting</u>

Let's face it, humans are not fans of the dark in general. This topic could span an entire chapter all by itself, but when talking about lighting, there are few requirements that we have. First, we need a hand held tactical light, a general flashlight (not the same thing), and something for area lighting, such as lighting a tent. For full disclosure, I have over a dozen flashlights.

For the tactical light, you need a small but very powerful flashlight (200-700 lumens) that you can carry on your belt or bag every day. This should be part of your EDC even before a WROL situation unfolds. Do not go with the 80s era, large Mag-Lights. While those are fine for a vehicle, you want something that can be carried with you everywhere. You don't know where you'll be when the power goes out. I've been inside some pretty sketchy locations in Detroit when the lights have gone off and a concealed belt-carried flashlight was a life-saver in finding my way out, and we aren't even in a WROL situation yet.

When selecting a tactical flashlight, spend the money to get a good one, you are betting your life on it. It's easy to buy the cheap "tactical lights" that are sold everywhere at low cost, including the gas station. Buy one that is intended to be used with a firearm. This is often overlooked, but true tactical lights are pressure sealed; cheap, gas station ones are not. When a firearm goes off right next to the cheap one, the glass or lighting element could shatter, leaving you without light when you need it most.

Features to look for in a tactical light are a minimum of 200 lumens, a "pressure switch" (allows you turn it on only for an instant), a strobe feature (can induce nausea and disorientation if shined in the eyes), and a strike bezel (allows you to strike an attacker with the flashlight in close quarters).

The second type of flashlight you need is a normal flashlight. You don't always want to throw light a mile and a half, and tactical lights are generally too focused and harsh to allow you to use them for everyday use. Find some type of quality, everyday flashlight, not the $2 plastic kind.

A good option here is the good old US Military Angle Head flashlight. It is high quality, and has a clip, allowing you to attach it your gear and see in front of you, hands free.   You could also clip it near the roof of your tent to light the tent.

Newer versions feature LED lights with variable brightness. These lights also come with various colored lenses for use for security. Red lenses give light that can't be seen from far away and help in reading maps at night. The newer versions are also made of aluminum, making them more sturdy, and some allow you to change light colors without changing lenses.

The third type of light we need is some type of lantern type area light. This is more of a work light or a comfort light. These come in a myriad of sizes and brightnesses. You'll need to shop around, but I'll cover a few good features to look for.

- Seek one that is rechargeable. You could leave it attached to a solar panel trickle-charge all day, and then use it all night.

- Hanger: Some type of hanging method should be attached to the light, allowing you to hang it from a height or over something you are working on.

- Multi-Use: There are several lights on the market that function as both a hand-held flashlight and as a lantern.

I didn't mention gas powered lanterns, like a Coleman, because in a WROL situation, you might not be able to get fuel. Here we are talking about the Base Line minimum standard.

<u>Optics - Day</u>

No matter what your imagined post-WROL role will be, you'll need the ability to see a distance away.

Binoculars are a required item, but how do we pick them out? There are a lot of people with a lot of different answers, but let's cover just the bare minimum.

First, higher magnification isn't always better. The higher the magnification, the smaller the "field of view" that you can see. Also, any movements you make are also magnified in the image you see, so the more shaky your image is. A standard 8 or 10 power set is good enough.

When looking at binoculars, you'll always see two numbers, like 8x25 or 12x40. The second number is diameter of the lens. You may think this is no big deal and more compact is the way to go, but if you intend to use the optics in low light, you want a larger number, because it's also indicative of the amount of light the binoculars gather.

In the same way that it amplifies the image visually, binoculars also gather light and can help you see in poor conditions, like rain, dusk, etc.

My personal solution is to carry a small compact set (8x25) on my chest rig, and a higher quality pair in Patrol Pack (16x32). For the purposes of this manual, that's good enough.

Don't be drawn into discussions about the country the "glass" came from and the brand names, those just get you to spend money for minor improvements in quality.

Another optic type to consider is a spotting scope. The same standards apply, and you'll want a decent one to use for observation posts. For spotting scopes, consider the platform (tripod) as just as important. The more stable you can make a spotting scope the better. As far as power, 20-40 times is a good start.

I also carry a 10x25 monocular on my chest rig (or Get Home Bag) as a quick way to check my route for movement or to investigate things glanced at a distance. It's a good way to get a quick read, and if I need to look closer, I can get out a better set of optics from my bag.
You can also be more discreet in an urban environment using a monocular than binoculars.

<u>Optics - Night</u>

I almost didn't include night optics, because we are only discussing the Base Line standard in this volume, but it is worth touching on briefly.

First, let's agree that we, most likely, are not going to be conducting offensive operations against a static enemy at night, so night optics are not an absolute requirement. I know that will generate some disagreement, but we have to be honest with ourselves; we aren't about to infiltrate a Chinese base, or sneak into a FEMA camp to liberate anyone.

Second, you need to know that ACTIVE night vision, where you are projecting an IR light forward, works BOTH WAYS. So, if we WERE to try and infiltrate that Chinese FOB or FEMA camp, they'd see you coming before you got within range of your night vision.

That being said, you can find passable night vision for your own use or at an observation post for under $200.

What do I mean by "passable night vision"? So many in preparedness talk as if the entire time will be spent fending off the hordes of barbarians, battling government troops, or repelling the Chinese armored cavalry. The truth is far less exciting.

Static security will be the norm and your intent won't be to gain contact or infiltrate at night, it will be to gain EARLY WARNING. A "passable" set of night vision would then not be best used to see actual people moving, which would have to be almost on top of you to see with night vision, but to detect OTHER PEOPLE using night vision, which can be done at great distances with even the most basic night vision.

For example, if I'm manning an OP, another group moving using night vision will appear like a flashlight in the distance via my own night optics. That's best use of night optics in the defense. You'll then be able to see where they are and if they get closer, raise the alarm. You'll be able to do this using PASSIVE night vision yourself, not projecting a beam and remaining unseen.

<u>Compass</u>

While we will discuss Land Navigation in a later volume, it's worth discussing desirable compass features here.

No matter what you envision post-WROL life to be like, you'll need a compass. The United States Armed Forces has the ability to shut off GPS signals anytime they want. They don't have the ability to the shift the polarity of the Earth.

Compasses have been used reliably for hundreds of years, so it's a great tool to have in a WROL situation.

The following features are an absolute must:

- Rotating bezel: To be able to navigate, you need to be able to adjust the compass markings.

- Straight edge with scale: For reading maps, plotting routes, or determining your location, it's important to be able make a straight line & measure distances.

- Degree Scale: A good compass should have a degree scale, cheap ones don't. The best kind have both degrees and mils.

- Luminous: You should be able to determine direction at night.

- Lanyard hole: A compass is so important that you need a way to keep from losing it. Using a dummy cord tied through the lanyard hole, you can secure the compass to your gear so that it can't be dropped.

Standard US Military compasses are a great option.

<u>Map Tools</u>

Paper maps are an absolute must, but with paper maps comes the need to protect them from the weather. We also may want the capability to write on the maps for documenting things we've seen or route planning.

US Military surplus map protectors are a good option, but hard to find. These are large zip-lock plastic sheets that you can put a map in, and then write on with dry/wet erase markers.

Another option is a product called a Battle Board. They are notebook holders with a polycarbonate window on the front that you can place a map behind. This protects the map and allows you to take notes or draw on the map with dry or wet erase markers. They are available in several sizes.

<u>Base Line Standard</u>

- Collapsible Shovel

- Hand Axe

- Tactical Light

- Standard Flashlight

- Lantern-Type light

- Day Optics (8x25 minimum)

- Compass

- Optional: Basic night vision optics

- Optional: Spotting scope

<u>Resources:</u>

BattleBoard   <u>www.battleboard.us</u>

Tactical Wisdom

Base Line Training Manual

Chapter 14

Functional Testing

*So that the Man of God may be thoroughly equipped
For every good work.*

2 Timothy 3:17

If you've made it this far, you gathered gear, assembled different bags, kits, and supplies, and you've gotten yourself started on a fitness plan. So, we're totally ready, right?

Wrong.

All the gear in the world doesn't do you any good if you don't know how to use it, and you aren't prepared until you've actually practiced something and tested it out.

It's one thing to set up your tent in the front yard, to test the batteries in your gear, try out the radios, and maybe test your camp stove. Those are all done under ideal conditions and in a secure environment.

How then, do we test our gear and abilities? Functional testing.

Functional testing is doing a full-on dress rehearsal and using our stuff with real-world consequences. By real-world consequences, I mean that if your sleeping system isn't right for conditions, you get cold, or if you can't light a fire, you go hungry; I don't mean you die alone on a mountaintop, just to be clear.

Functional testing could best described as a field training exercise. We will begin with short tests to acclimate ourselves, then build to bigger and longer tests, eventually culminating in full group weekend tests. These are a great way to learn what works, what doesn't work, how to best adjust our gear load, and train on practical skills.

As a culture, we've become soft. We are less likely to go outdoors and do things if the weather is cold, or it's raining, or it's snowing. In a post-event world, we won't have that luxury.

Post-event, things will still need to be done if it's raining, especially security tasks. We're going to accomplish two things with functional testing:

1. Test our gear and carrying methods.

2. Acclimate ourselves to the outdoors and the climate.

This might seem silly, but we have to be honest. Western culture is used to a controlled climate. We use air conditioning in the heat and heat when it's cold. We have to ease ourselves back into the natural world.

I live in Michigan, and it amazes me how many people there are who live here that can't handle the cold. They've allowed themselves to become so used to a controlled climate, that they can't regulate their own reactions.

First Step Drill

Just like you can't go from sitting on the couch to winning a marathon, we can't just go from sitting on the couch to living in the field for days at a time. There is a building process, and we'll start with small steps.

The first step is grab one of your bags, either the Get Home Bag or the EDC/Patrol Bag, and go somewhere that you can hike. Hike for at least one hour.

You have to do this in every weather condition, so don't skip it if it's raining, snowing, or too hot.

While we're on the topic of it being too hot, let's talk for a second about how you should dress in a preparedness situation. You should be wearing long pants and a long sleeve shirt. If you are actually in the woods or engaged in anything that could result in hostile action, your sleeves should be rolled down fully.

Survival in any environment involves environmental risks and in a post-event world, small cuts and insect bites can be deadly, due to the risk of infection. Sunburn, in a post-event world, can also be deadly.

Proper footwear is vital in a WROL situation. A good practice is to buy several pairs of comfortable, quality footwear now, and put them away as preparedness supplies.

An article of clothing to avoid for survival is denim. First, denim isn't great for a full range of motion. Second, when wet, denim shrinks and becomes stiff. Third, it takes forever for denim to dry naturally.

<u>The Lunch Test</u>

After just getting used to moving in gear in the outdoors, it's time for a bit more of a test.

Get into your food supplies and get out some of your portable food. A note about this is that when preparing, don't just buy food, buy meals. As an example, buy a can of Spanish Rice and a pouch of chicken breast. You can put them together and you have a meal.

Put the food and whatever your portable cooking system is in the bag, whether it's just fire starting gear, a canteen cup stove and heating tablets, or a backpacking stove. Don't forget water.

Hike out into the woods for about an hour, then set yourself up in a secure rest area. By secure, we mean off the main trail you are using, in a covered and concealed area. Set this site up as you would in a real-world situation:

- Find a concealed area.

- Establish a hide/security position, which you should be doing anytime you halt while moving.

- Set up a concealed location for your bag.

- If you brought a radio along (which you should for real training), set up the radio including any higher antennas you plan to use in static positions (like tossing your roll-up antenna into a tree).

- Clear a cooking area.

Once you have the site set up, get out your cooking system and food, then prepare the meal and enjoy it. Once you've gotten the items out of the bag, close the bag, it 's a good habit to start.

A cold camp lunch where you don't cook is fine, but make it a real-life WROL type lunch. In other words, you won't be making a ham & Swiss on rye with mayo in a collapse environment. You may have a chicken salad pouch on MRE bread or crackers, for example.

After eating the field lunch, sterilize the site, packing your trash out with you. In a true WROL situation, you would most likely bury your trash inside a plastic baggie, as long as you aren't being pursued or trying not to leave any trace.
Remember, we only want to take out what we need from our pack, so don't fully unpack.

Throughout the exercise, try to keep your gear in such a way that you could put it away and be moving in less than 2 minutes.

Do this exercise in all weather conditions. For a true challenge, try doing this in an urban setting. You can find a neighborhood park or a drain area where you can do this exercise.

After getting used to this, start extending the length of the test. One of the biggest misconceptions people have about WROL life is the amount of time they will be able to spend moving or the distance that they cover on foot in one day. By extending the length of these trips, you're developing your ability to move distances at speed while carrying a load.

<u>Overnight Test</u>

Once we've done the first two tests, it's time to plan an overnight test with your sleep system and your planned field shelter, whether it's a tarp or a tent.

When planning this, you want to be far enough from home that you won't be tempted to just rely on your resources at home. You want somewhere you can drive to, but don't drive directly to the camp site, drive to a parking area, where you will then ruck your way into the overnight stay area.

Hike in, moving tactically, and establish your camp with security and concealment in mind. You don't want to arrive at an overnight location much more than one hour before dark.

Once you get to the camp site, the overnight test has these steps:

1. Set up a security overwatch post, looking over the most likely avenue of approach.

2. Decide where your sleeping area will be and where you'll stash your pack overnight.

3. Set up your radio, including any antennas. As a bonus, you can test making contact with another member of your team via radio or practice tuning in an amateur station for news.

4. Establish a cat-hole waste area a good distance away from the main site.

5. Set up a cooking system and prepare your evening meal. Secure all cooking gear after eating; don't leave it out until morning. We're going for real-world training and we want to be able to move out quickly at all times.

6. Just before settling down to sleep, set up your sleeping system and shelter, trying to have as small of a footprint as possible, and being as quiet as possible.

7. In the morning, take down the shelter and secure the sleeping system before doing anything else.

8. When you conduct "self-administration" like cleaning and brushing teeth, resist the urge get out all the supplies at once. Remember, we aren't just camping.

9. After taking down the shelter and completing administrative tasks, make your morning meal.

10. The last step is to sterilize the site, reducing any signs that you were ever in the area.

11. Move out and return to the vehicle.

As you can see, this is a serious test. It will truly let you know if you are actually prepared, or just having an unrealistic hobby.

Strive for realism. There will be no campfire, no cold ones relaxing. All cooking should be done before dark, so that the fire can't be seen from a distance.

If you hear something during the night, run it as a security drill: Get out of the shelter and sleep system quietly, and get to your security position and observe.

We will get more into patrol base operations in other volumes.

<u>Group Overnight Test</u>

The natural progression will then be to get your whole group together to do a group overnight test. There are only a couple of alterations to the test.

1. Half of the party mans security posts, while the other half eats and sets up their shelter, and then they switch roles.

2. The entire party mans the security perimeter, watching outward, during dusk until just after full dark.

3. With a team of more than 4, you will set up a watch schedule, with someone up and watching the most

likely avenue of approach all night, rotating among the group in 1-2 hour shifts.

4. Just before morning twilight, the entire group should be gotten up to man the security perimeter during twilight. This isn't done with a loud announcement, the person on watch quietly wakes everyone.

5. Half the team maintains watch while the other half does the morning routine of shelter take down, administration, and eating, then the other half.

6. The whole groups checks the site for sterilization, before moving out.

Again, there is no large "hang-out" campfire, we're not camping. The security work may seem over-the-top, but in a true WROL situation, there will be bad people out along with hungry and desperate people.

<u>Full Exercise</u>

Once the whole team is comfortable with this, plan a full-on bug out exercise. Have some fun with this and strive for realism. Write an actual scenario out for everyone.

While it's a planned drill, and everyone will know ahead of time, so it's not a true "drill", try to set time limits. For example, each person must meet at the first rally point within 15 minutes of a certain time or be left behind and have to catch up.

Establish a meeting place and as people arrive, position the vehicles as you will have them for the vehicle movement portion. In other words, set them up in a convoy arrangement. Don't just let people sit in their cars or hang out while waiting for others to arrive, we are training for a real world emergency, so as teams arrive, place their vehicles in the formation, then assign them a sector to face outward on foot and pull security on.

Once the whole group is present, conduct a radio check and move out. Try and maintain your convoy integrity while moving.

When you arrive where you are parking to transition to foot movement, remember that we are still running a drill. Assign half the team to cover the perimeter, while the rest unpacks & readies their gear, then switch. There should be a time limit on this.

As soon as everyone is geared up, move out on foot tactically, and run the same drill as the overnight.

If it's a weekend long drill, change locations via foot movement during the day, even if it's only a short distance, so that we are practicing establishing a secure camp and practicing secure movement.

When returning to the vehicles, the drill isn't over. Practice re-boarding vehicles and securing the site.

You'll find it more enjoyable this way.

<u>After-Action Reviews</u>

After every training event, even solo ones, hold an after-action review.

During this review, discuss what worked well, what didn't work well, and what changes need to be made for full readiness. It's not a bad idea to write this down so that you can follow through on needed changes.

Don't pull punches and don't be defensive, the purpose isn't to decide who was best or worst, the purpose to improve everyone's readiness.

<u>Base Line Standard</u>

- Conduct the First Step Test in all environmental conditions.

- Conduct the Lunch Test at least once per month.

- Conduct a solo Overnight Test at lest once per quarter (all four seasons).

- If you have a team, conduct the Team Overnight Test at least once every 6 months, although quarterly is better.

- If you have a team, conduct the Team Full Exercise at least once per year.

Tactical Wisdom

Base Line Training Manual

Chapter 15

Maintaining The Baseline

Therefore keep watch,
Because you do not know the day or the hour.

Matthew 25:13

Now that you've gathered the bare minimum gear, built your bags, gotten fit, and organized your team, what's next?

After conducting the most basic of training as listed in the Functional Training chapter, it's now time to ensure that we maintain the baseline. In other words, you should never fall below the minimum standards outlined in the Base Line Training Manual.

Since we don't know when an incident or a complete collapse will occur, once we've established our baseline, we will need to maintain our readiness. Without an imminent threat, many people find it hard to justify keeping ready, but we need to.

The first thing we need to do is understand that preparedness supplies are for PREPAREDNESS. With the exception of first aid kits, we don't dig into our preparedness supplies for daily use.

Anything that you use, whether for a training event, or used first aid supplies, should be replenished immediately from your stocks. I know that with first aid supplies, it's tempting to wait until you use a whole package of band-aids or whatever, but once again, we don't know when an event could occur and we will need those supplies immediately. Restock as you use.

<u>Weekly Maintenance Tasks</u>

Each week, you should update your situational awareness. Conduct research on local news and national news to ensure that you are as aware as possible of the current local, state, and national/international situation.

On a weekly basis, check all flashlights and radios to ensure that they are fully charged. You may be tempted to make this a monthly task, but we don't know when they'll be needed, and being unable to communicate & in the dark can completely demoralize you at the outset of an event.

<u>Monthly Maintenance Tasks</u>

About once a month, check each bag to make sure that it's still fully stocked and ready to go. You could make this easier by checking one bag each week.

Another monthly task is food rotation. Food should be stocked with the nearest expiration dates first. Once a month, check dates, and then move things expiring within the next 3 months to your regular food supplies and put it on a replenishment list for your preparedness food supplies.

Once a month you should take a long ruck with your Full Ruck. During regular fitness training, you should use your EDC/Patrol Bag, but at least once a month put on the Full Ruck and do a long one.

You should hold some type of team meeting, whether virtual or in-person at a minimum of once per month. This could even be just a quick touch-base, or a full get-together event.

I know that we didn't discuss firearms in this manual, and that's intentional, but you should conduct firearms training once a month, at a minimum. Any physical skill is lost if you don't use it and firearms manipulation is no different.

Notice also the use of the word "training" and not "shooting". Shooting holes in paper on a stationary flat range has little real application to defensive firearms use. Find somewhere that will let you conduct fire and movement, as well as other skills that require breaking flat range rules. Safety is still vital.

<u>Quarterly Maintenance Tasks</u>

At least quarterly, your entire team should meet for some type of training event. Use the ideas presented in Functional Testing.

As each season arrives, go through the bags and adjust for seasonal factors. For example, you don't need a heavy sleeping bag in summer. You may need to add a sweater or heavy coat for winter, etc.

Also on a quarterly basis, you will need to check out all of the planned routes you have. There may be new construction on roads, exits may be closed, or that wooded area you were going to traverse may now be developed.

Check your preparedness goals and assess where you on them each quarter. If you have met all your current goals, establish new ones that enable you to continue to develop yourself.

Update your Area Study with more current data.

<u>Annual Tasks</u>

Each year, make a list of training goals and check your progress on last year's goals. These should be skill-based and focused on no-technology skills.
<u>Closing</u>

Remember that this book is just the base line. These are the bare minimum for preparedness. This is by no means the end.

As we go down this path together, alway make sure that you meet the Base Line Standard at the end of each chapter. There will be additional volumes that address specific tasks and goals that will be in addition to the standards herein.

<u>Base Line Standard</u>

- Check each bag every month to ensure that it is fully stocked and ready to go.

- Hold monthly team meetings or events.

- Rotate food stocks.

- Hold at least quarterly group training events.

- Adjust your bag/pack contents for seasonal issues.

- At least quarterly, review your routes.

- Set and assess goals.

Tactical Wisdom

Base Line Training Manual

Warrior Study: Elijah

This information first appeared as blog post on my website, tactical-wisdom.com, where I share preparedness advice based on God's Ultimate Tactical Handbook.

This study is of Elijah, who could best be described as an intelligence officer for God. He conducted intelligence operations, built a subversive resistance, hid dissenters from the authorities, and gave us some good preparedness advice.

I hope this story helps tie together the chapters of this book.

Here it is:

There is a lot of preparedness and tactical knowledge in the Bible, and that's where the motivation for this book comes from. Hidden inside the Bible are a lot of great adventure stories that rival the Lord of the Rings, but you have you to know where to find them.

The story of Elijah is one of those. His story is one of wilderness survival, resisting a tyrannical government, intelligence gathering, and war. I know, your pastor doesn't tell you that in the snippets he gives you on Sunday, but hold, on, we're going for a ride.

I am going to briefly recap his story, and illustrate the preparedness and tactical truths that are just as valid today as we go along. Historically, we know that the one major battle depicted did in fact occur between King Ahab and King Ben-Hadad in about 857 BC, so these truths are over 2,000 years old and still valid.

This story is found in 1 Kings 17-21.

First, Elijah delivers an ultimatum and warning to the King, Ahab, right at the outset. Elijah, being a smart and prepared young man, knows that it's a good idea when you put the government on notice, to immediately clear the area.

He immediately fled from the capitol, and went and hid in a ravine. He choose a ravine because it had a solid water supply. In verse 17:6, God tells Elijah "I have commanded the ravens to bring you food". Now, the Bible is an odd book, because sometimes you're meant to take it literally, and sometimes, you aren't. This notice from God was basically saying that the Elijah was to live off the land. Ravens are scavengers and that's the example for Elijah. The water eventually dried up, so Elijah had to move on.

There are a couple of lessons for us here:

1. Pick a location with access to water.

2. Have the skills to enable you to live off the land.

3. If conditions (like access to water) change, be prepared to change locations.

I always say that skills beat stuff (gear) every day. I didn't say, "Bring all the gear to live off the land", I said have the skills.

In Chapter 18, we learn about a man named Obadiah. While Elijah was playing Ted Kaczynski Mountain-Man, chilling out with the ravens, Jezebel had ordered her guards (the police) to round up all the Jewish followers of God (sound familiar?). When Obadiah saw this happening, he gathered 100 of them to hide.

But…Obadiah was SMART. He found 2 caves, and hid 50 of the people in each cave and kept them supplied with food and water. That way, if a cave was found, they weren't all found.

Sounds like a principle we can use today:

1. Establish multiple bug-out locations.

2. For supplies, never put them all in one cache, in case it is found or seized (Yes, the Defense Production Act allows them to be seized).

3. If forced to, reveal only one location, which will allow you to preserve at least 50% of your supplies, more if you have more than 2 locations.

4. You could theoretically have a planned "surrender" stash for exactly this purpose.

5. Have a network or plan for resupply as needed.

Shortly after Elijah returned, Jezebel sent him a messenger. The messenger advised Elijah that she was going to hunt him down and kill him. Doesn't that sound exactly like the rhetoric we're hearing right now? Anyway, on hearing this, Elijah immediately showed his wisdom and tactical acumen by immediately leaving the area.

1. Listen to what people tell you they're going to do. Take them at their word and prepare accordingly.

2. Never accept the fight on someone else's terms, if you can avoid it. You pick the time and place, not the opposition.

Elijah fled, but this time, he wasn't prepared. He ran out into the wilderness with no supplies and quickly got overwhelmed. He laid down under a tree and asked God to take his life.

Now, God sent an Angel to feed Elijah in verse 19:7, but you and I can't plan on that. After he ate what the Angel brought (This Angel was the first Uber Eats delivery ever recorded, by the way), Elijah felt better and made a concrete plan.

Our learnings here:

1. Never plan to move without food & water.

2. Your "bug-out bag" or "5 minute bag", whatever you call it, should contain at least some food and water, and a means to get more food and purify more water.

3. In verse 17:6, the Angel LITERALLY tells Elijah he needs food & water for strength for his journey, and so do you.

4. Every situation looks better after a bite to eat.

5. If you don't have food in a mobile format to allow you to live long enough to get to your 25-year food stash, it doesn't matter how much you have stored in that cabin in the woods.

6. Never just flee blindly, always have a plan & destination in mind.

After Elijah made it to his bug out location (a cave in the mountains), he was sent on an intelligence mission to gather forces to launch an attack against evil King Ahab.

Elijah set out and gathered a coalition of 33 Kings to come together and fight the battle.

1. The enemy of your enemy might not exactly be your friend, but he is your ALLY.

2. Build coalitions of nearby mutual aid groups or residents to band together in the event a larger force is needed for defense.

3. Establish a clear chain of command, because this large force, LOST the battle ultimately because each King had his own goals, rather than a mutual goal together.

In Chapter 20, The Battle of Samaria, which occurred in 857 BC plays out, and there are lessons in it. Israel won the battle, despite being overwhelmingly outnumbered (7,000 versus about 200,000).

But first, before the battle, Ben-Hadad sent a list of demands to Ahab. While the demands were tough; all his gold & silver, and his best wives (I wonder who made the cut, and how happy the ones he kept were at not thought of as being the best), Ahab agreed. The next day, Ben-Hadad sent more demands, which were too excessive, and Ahab refused.

1. Appeasement to demands will only get you more demands, until you have nothing left.

2. The Munich Agreement of 1938 is a classic example of this.

The lessons learned in the battle are:

1. The Arameans were not surprised because they had scouts out watching the enemy.

2. Always establish observation posts/listening posts and send out scouts, even if you can only send 2 people.

3. Israel won with a small force, because they gave full authority to conduct the battle to "junior officers", rather than the generals. The Arameans didn't.

4. Always empower small unit leaders.

In Chapter 21, a man named Naboth owned some land that King Ahab wanted, but he refused to sell it to him. Jezebel sent some government agents, who arranged a meeting. At the meeting, they sat Naboth between some known criminals, who were told to accuse Naboth of conspiring with them (Man, does that sounds familiar?). Naboth was arrested and killed.

1.   Entrapment to meet government goals has existed as long as man has established governments.

2.   The more tyrannical the government becomes, the more it uses informants and undercover agents (Read that again. Then again.)

3.   Don't trust "new " people that no one else knows.

4.   Vet anyone who wants to be affiliated with you.

5.   If anyone starts talking about taking illegal action or building illegal items, RUN. Cut them off completely.

Thanks for bearing with me and listening to the tale of Elijah and his band of subversive agents. There is much more to the story, but this is the part that applied to our topics.

I hope these tales gave you a couple of ideas to help you prepare.

www.ingramcontent.com/pod-product-compliance
Lightning Source LLC
Chambersburg PA
CBHW060048260726

48658CB00004B/1226